WOMEN and the Democratic Party

WOMEN and the Democratic Party

The Evolution of EMILY's List

Jamie Pamelia Pimlott

Politics, Institutions, and Public Policy in America series
Series editors: Scott A. Frisch and Sean Q. Kelly

CAMBRIA PRESS

Amherst, New York

Copyright 2010 Jamie Pamelia Pimlott

All rights reserved
Printed in the United States of America

No part of this publication may be reproduced, stored in or introduced into a retrieval system, or transmitted, in any form, or by any means (electronic, mechanical, photocopying, recording, or otherwise), without the prior permission of the publisher.

Requests for permission should be directed to:
permissions@cambriapress.com, or mailed to:
Cambria Press
20 Northpointe Parkway, Suite 188
Amherst, NY 14228

Library of Congress Cataloging-in-Publication Data

Pimlott, Jamie Pamelia.
  Women and the Democratic Party: the evolution of Emily's List / Jamie Pamelia Pimlott.
     p. cm.
  Includes bibliographical references and index.
  ISBN 978-1-60497-655-7 (alk. paper)
 1. Emily's List (Network) 2. Women in politics—United States. 3. Democratic Party (U.S.) 4. Political action committees—United States. I. Title.

  HQ1236.5.U5P56 2010
  324'.40973—dc22

2009042786

*To Pamelia—my most precious gift
and the most beautiful, intelligent, female
pro-choice Democrat in the world*

Table of Contents

List of Tables and Figure	ix
Acknowledgments	xiii
Chapter 1: An Introduction to EMILY's List	1
Chapter 2: The Second Wave and EMILY's List	13
Chapter 3: The Transformation of EMILY's List	41
Chapter 4: Members and Their Organizational Roles	85
Chapter 5: Candidates and the Organization	117
Chapter 6: EMILY's List and Its "Mojo"	135
Chapter 7: Conclusion	147
Appendices	163
A. Coding Guide for Emily's List Mailings	163
B. Data Collapsing and Coding	166
C. Donor Breakdown According to Election Cycle and State	171
References	173
Index	203

LIST OF TABLES AND FIGURE

Table 2.1. Receipts and candidate contributions by select women's PACs, 1980–1984.   21

Table 2.2. Receipts and candidate contributions from EMILY's List and select women's PACs, 1986–2008.   30

Table 2.3. Candidate contributions (including bundled money) from EMILY's List and select women's PACs, 1986–2008.   31

Table 2.4. Money given by women's PACs to national political parties, 1980–2008.   34

Figure 3.1. Receipts to EMILY's List, 1986–2008.   50

Table 3.1. EMILY's List PAC contributions to candidates (direct and in-kind) and bundled money, 1986–2008.   56

Table 3.2. Number of candidates endorsed by EMILY's List by primary date and outcome, 2000–2008.   58

Table 3.3. EMILY's List WOMEN VOTE! projects, 1994–2008.   65

Table 3.4.	EMILY's List non-federal expenditures, 1986–2008.	66
Table 3.5.	EMILY's List political opportunity activities, 2002–2008.	68
Table 3.6.	Receipts to EMILY's List 527, 2002–2008.	71
Table 4.1.	EMILY's List donors by sex, 2000–2008.	94
Table 4.2.	Occupational status of EMILY's List donors, 2000–2008.	96
Table 4.3.	EMILY's List members by state, 2000–2008.	99
Table 4.4.	EMILY's List members and endorsed candidates by state, 2000–2008.	102
Table 4.5.	Percentage of new and repeat donors to ELIST by election cycle, 2002–2008.	105
Table 4.6.	Amount of money given to EMILY's List and candidates (bundled) by election cycle, donor sex, and donor type, 2002–2008.	107
Table 4.7.	Conversion of Newbies by election cycle, 2002–2006.	109

Table 5.1.	EMILY's List endorsement by seat status, chamber, and year, 2000–2008.	119
Table 5.2.	Logistic regression: Who is EMILY's List more likely to support?	124
Table 5.3.	Predicting EMILY's List dollars.	129

Acknowledgments

This book is the product of years of work, frustration, hope, persistence and help from others. I must begin by thanking Sean Kelly and all the people at Cambria Press—thank you for believing in me and this book. I would like to thank all of the members of Congress, members of EMILY's List, and Founding Mothers who spoke to me about EMILY's List over the past five years. I would like to thank Karen O'Connor and Sarah Brewer for introducing me to several important persons in D.C. that helped expand this project. I would like to thank David Reilly and Nancy McGlen for the support and encouragement as I struggled to balance family, teaching, administrative duties and completing the manuscript. My thanks also go out to the Research Council and the EVPAA's office at Niagara University as well as Lawrence C. Dodd, Margaret Conway, Dan Smith, Beth Rosenson, Lynn Leverty and Kendal Broad at the University of Florida. This book began as a paper for Dan Smith's Campaign Finance course—half a decade later it has become a book because of the teaching, encouragement, and suggestions of all of you. I would also like to thank my former colleagues at the Campaign Finance Institute—Michael J. Malbin, Brendan Glavin, Wesley Joe—all of you played an integral role in my formation as a scholar and a person. To Kara, thanks for keeping me sane! And finally to Shawn Davis and Jennifer Chmura for all the hard work and laughs—you two are irreplaceable as research assistants and as friends!

There are five persons, however, who must be thanked individually. The first is Larry Dodd. Words cannot express how thankful I am that Leslie suggested I go and talk to you eight years ago. Out of that conversation I gained a professor, an advisor, a mentor, and a friend. Every time I have a student come into my office to talk I find myself asking them how they are doing and getting to know them—I became a much better teacher and mentor because of you. And every time I stand up in front of a class and get excited because I'm talking about Congress, its puzzles, its evolution, its power-that too is because of you. Thank you for showing me my academic path. I only hope I can make you proud.

To my parents, words cannot express how much love I have for you. I'll never forget pulling the all-nighter(s) in the loft during the summer of 2009 in order to get the revisions finished. I have always done my best work sitting in pajamas while you two buzzed around the house. You taught me to never give up, regardless of the barriers I faced, and there have been many. I would like to think that this book is a testament to those teachings. Dad, without our political debates, I doubt I would have found my calling. I promise to catch up on the news immediately! Mom, words cannot express the debts I owe you. Over a decade ago,

Acknowledgments

I said you were the 'Wind Beneath My Wings'—thanks for teaching me how to fly and for always catching me when I fall.

To Dana and Pamie: I cannot imagine my life without either of you in it. Pamie, being your mom is the most precious gift I could ever receive—you are an amazing, beautiful, intelligent, hilarious girl with the sweetest heart I have ever seen. You grew up listening to me talk about EMILY's List and patiently waiting for me to finish the project. Sweets, it is finally done! Dana, I never imagined I would find a man as wonderful as you. You are my best friend, my intellectual equal (if not superior), my soulmate, and the love of my life. You have always been there to celebrate with me and to wipe my tears. We've faced incredible adversity over the last seven years, but we have always made it through because we love one another. Thank you for reading version after version, for putting up with my snarks, and for keeping me (and us) moving forward. While this book is the result of the guidance, teaching, and love of all these individuals, any mistakes herein are strictly my own.

WOMEN
and the
Democratic
Party

CHAPTER 1

AN INTRODUCTION TO EMILY'S LIST

EMILY's List made the "big time" in 2008, achieving national notoriety for its endorsement of Hillary Clinton's presidential bid just hours after she announced her candidacy in January 2007. In her endorsement, President and founder Ellen R. Malcolm promised to put the full weight of the organization behind Clinton:

> As Sen. Clinton begins her historic journey, EMILY's List will be with her every step of the way—raising early money from our grassroots donor network of tens of thousands of EMILY's List members, using our vast political resources to help her build a strong national campaign, and mobilizing millions of women voters through our groundbreaking WOMEN VOTE! program to support her and every Democrat on the ticket in 2008. (Malcolm 2007)

In the months that followed, EMILY's List staff and advisers became regulars on MSNBC, *Larry King Live*, and CNN. By June 2008, EMILY's List had bundled almost half a million dollars to Clinton's presidential campaign and spent untold amounts on "get out the vote" (GOTV) efforts to bring Democratic women to the polls during the primary season.

Given this investment, when Clinton withdrew from the race in June 2008 after a long and sometimes bitter primary battle for the Democratic nomination, some asserted that Clinton's loss, while not the fault of EMILY's List, "calls into question the very core of EMILY's List's strategy" and thus the continued relevance of the organization (Vaida and Skalka 2008). However, Malcolm, while certainly disappointed with the outcome of the Democratic primary, redirected the attention of the organization's members and the public to the battles that remained: "The organization is on track this cycle to raise more than the $46 million in PAC and soft money it took in during the 2006 cycle" (Vaida and Skalka 2008). With those funds, Malcolm and ELIST had work to do, namely helping elect female pro-choice Democratic candidates up and down the ticket and helping elect a Democrat to the White House.

The endorsement of Hillary Clinton marked the organization's first real foray into presidential politics. Since its inception in 1985 as a political action committee (PAC), EMILY's List has focused on helping elect female pro-choice Democratic candidates to Congress and state/local office. In the early years, its activity centered on providing select female candidates with "seed" money, soliciting bundled checks from the organization's membership very early in the electoral cycle (pre-primary) in order to help viable female candidates circumvent well-known fundraising obstacles. Its success in bundling money to its candidates became ELIST's claim to fame, but in subsequent decades, a focus on its bundling prowess and its formal PAC status has led to a certain type of myopia vis-à-vis the organization's influence. Although EMILY's List began as and remains a non-connected PAC, categorizing it as such is reductionist.

Today, EMILY's List is much more than a PAC. Rather, over the past quarter of a century, EMILY's List has morphed into a multipronged influence organization that functions as a PAC, an interest group, a party adjunct, and a campaign organization. Its impact can be seen in the voting booth, in state and local governments, in the U.S. Congress, and even in the White House. In fact, there are few political theaters where EMILY's List has not become a major player. But this outcome was far from preordained, and thus, the goal of this book is to shed light on ELIST's transformation from a PAC to a multipronged influence organization.

Certain factors are critical to ELIST's transformation, not the least of which is Ellen Malcolm. From all accounts, Malcolm did not set out at an early age to become one of the top political strategists in the nation; she was rather reserved and kept her status as the heiress to the IBM fortune a tightly guarded secret. However, by the early 1990s, Malcolm had emerged an entrepreneurial leader who possessed the skills, social network, education, wealth, passion, and strategic vision necessary to catapult herself and EMILY's List into a position of influence and power in American politics.

MALCOLM: THE ULTIMATE IN TUPPERWARE SALES

EMILY's List began as a pseudo Tupperware party, but instead of a group of apolitical housewives discussing the merits of resealable containers and trading meatloaf recipes, the organization brought together groups of politically savvy women to discuss poll numbers, campaign platforms, and voter outreach efforts.[1] Like a typical Tupperware party, the guests in Malcolm's home that first night pulled out their checkbooks, but this time they were writing checks to support an idea—EMILY's List. The name stood for the group's mission: Early Money Is Like Yeast (it makes the dough rise).

Malcolm and the other Founding Mothers, well-versed in the realities of politics, wrote letters to everyone in their Rolodexes, telling them about their new group and encouraging them to join for a yearly fee of $100 to cover administrative costs. The leadership of the group identified viable female pro-choice, pro-ERA Democratic candidates and sent information about the candidate and the race to group members. Members promised to choose at least two endorsed candidates and send each a check of $100 or more. They were also encouraged to forward information about the group and its candidates to friends who were sympathetic to the organization's mission.

From these rather humble beginnings, the organization steadily grew. By 1988, the organization bundled over $650,000 to their list of recommended female candidates.[2] By 1992, it became the premier women's PAC, surpassing the other more established women's PACs. In 1994 EMILY's List began its work as a campaign organization, providing professional training to women who wanted to become campaign professionals and providing candidate training to female pro-choice women who wanted to run for office. By 1996, EMILY's List used data acquired through the *Women's Monitor* to microtarget and organize women at the mass level. These data became the basis of ELIST's WOMEN VOTE! program. These "get out the vote" (GOTV) efforts, combined with regular transfers of funds (from EMILY's List to the Democratic Party committees and vice versa), helped strengthen the ties between EMILY's List and the Democratic Party. Over the next few years, EMILY's List would become a key part of the Democratic Party coalition. In 2001 the organization took another transformative step, expanding its influence at the state level through the Political Opportunity Program (POP).

As the organization expanded and the pool of female Democratic pro-choice candidates grew, the scope of its campaign activities and party adjunct activities expanded as well, leading to the creation of several departments within the organization. As membership numbers have soared, the organization has stayed true to its PAC roots, bundling money to candidates, but has also been able to expand its PAC activity. As members give more money directly to the organization, ELIST has provided candidates with more direct and in-kind contributions from the PAC, and has recently spent considerable sums on independent expenditures. In recent years, EMILY's List has also proven to be adept at the "inside game" of lobbying. In the late 1990s, it began to engage in "traditional" interest-group activity, pressuring legislators to oppose the passage of restrictive campaign finance law.[3] In 2005 it filed suit against the Federal Election Commission over the regulation of 527 activities; in late September 2009, the U.S. District Court for the District of Columbia ruled in ELIST's favor (Malcolm 2009).

EMILY's List's successful transformation from donor network to multipronged influence organization has made it *the* model that many different types of groups and entities have tried to replicate. Yet for the most part, scholars and journalists, while acknowledging the tremendous success of EMILY's List in raising money from contributors, underestimate the scope and importance of the organization. Although EMILY's List *is* the premier women's PAC, providing candidates with early money is not what led reporters and pundits to refer to Ellen Malcolm, founder and president of EMILY's List, as the "queenmaker" of the Democratic Party (Spake 1988). Rather, it is the additional things that EMILY's List does *in combination with* its role as a women's PAC—particularly its ability to adapt to the changing political environment—that makes it so important. Only by understanding the distinct yet intricately connected activity of EMILY's List's multiple prongs can we understand how it has become such a critical player in American politics.

The stories of Malcolm and EMILY's List are intertwined. Some wonder what will happen to the organization when Malcolm steps away—a very appropriate question given the critical role she continues to play in the organization, and one that I address at several points in this text. However, those seeking a biography of Ellen Malcolm will be disappointed. Likewise, the book is not a history of the liberal feminist women's movement, although the movement's successes and especially its failures are part of this organization's origins, its mission, and its appeal. Malcolm, the liberal feminist women's movement, the rise of modern campaigning, the increasing relevance of money in electoral politics, the battle for partisan control of Congress and the White House—all of these various threads are part of the story. An examination of the origins of the organization; its leadership, membership, and candidates; and the impact of these on the electoral system and our institutions of government, especially the U.S. Congress, will make it clear that EMILY's List is much more than a women's PAC. By the end, readers will understand the transformative process that took place vis-à-vis EMILY's List, but readers will also gain insight into the structure and workings of contemporary interest groups, influence organization, and identity politics.

The Second Wave Feminist Movement and the Emergence of EMILY's List

After a brief review of the pertinent literature, I discuss how the women's movement set the stage for the formation of EMILY's

List. During the 1970s, women were faced with a series of challenges that forced them to take a stand on issues heretofore deemed personal and private; thus, the personal *became* political.[4] Issues such as abortion, education, employment, marriage, and children divided women from men *and* divided women from women. These issues even divided organizations (Barakso 2005). However, by the mid-1970s, the liberal feminist women's movement reached critical mass and became strong enough to maximize on the political opportunities available (Costain 1992). One of these political opportunities was the ability of groups to form PACs.

The arrival of PACs on the political stage was serendipitous for women. The second part of chapter 2 provides a brief history of the first two women's PACs: the National Women's Political Caucus (NWPC) and the Women's Campaign Fund (WCF). I explore the impact of these PACs before the formation of EMILY's List and then compare the three (NWPC, WCF, and EMILY's List) in terms of structure and impact through the 1992 election. It was that election that changed the trajectory of EMILY's List. Not only did EMILY's List become the leading women's PAC, but the 1992 election also set the stage for Malcolm's plan of making EMILY's List into a "full-service political organization."[5]

EMILY's List Is Transformed

I begin chapter 3 with a discussion of women as candidates and the obstacles they faced in spite their apparent success in the 1992 election. It is far from coincidental that when EMILY's List planned its post-1992 transformation, it focused on the very cornerstones that scholars identified as inhibiting women's success in the electoral arena. Ellen Malcolm's entrepreneurial leadership is critical to this strategy; she has kept the organization agile and dynamic, leading its expansion into new arenas of influence, while simultaneously keeping it firmly rooted to its mission and history.

MEMBERS AND THEIR ORGANIZATIONAL ROLES

In this chapter, I explore the relationship between the members and the organization. EMILY's List membership grew exponentially from 1986 to the present day. The organization brings in over $25 million in receipts and the vast majority of its membership is female—yet the conventional wisdom is that women do not contribute to politics often and especially do not give large amounts (Francia et al. 2003). How, then, does EMILY's List get women to donate so much money, and who are these ELISTERs? Are they simply a network of loyal donors, "political elite" women located in the Beltway? Or is the organization, in fact, a broad-based entity that attracts men and women from all over the country who give both large and small amounts, driven to become members for a variety of reasons?

CANDIDATES AND THE ORGANIZATION

According to the organization's literature, candidates endorsed by EMILY's List have four things in common: they are female pro-choice Democrats who are viable candidates. In chapter 5, I explore the relationship between candidates and the organization. EMILY's List supported all but a few of the Democratic women who have made it into the U.S. Congress since 1986.[6] What is the secret to EMILY's List's success? How does the organization assess viability, and how has that changed over time? Does EMILY's List follow an access-oriented strategy, which would fit with their interest-group activities, or does it follow an election-oriented strategy, dictated by its status as a women's PAC? Furthermore, has it remained true to its mission of providing "early" money, or as it's evolved, has it become more conservative about risking money? Finally, what impact does an EMILY's List endorsement have on election outcomes? Just *how* successful is it?

EMILY's LIST AND ITS "MOJO"

The focus of chapter 6 is the 2008 election, specifically EMILY's List's entrée into presidential politics and what that meant for the organization, its mission, its leadership, its members, and its future. After its early endorsement of Hillary Rodham Clinton in the Democratic presidential primary and the battle that followed, some perceived that the fate of EMILY's List was inextricably tied to Clinton's candidacy. Did Clinton's concession also mark the decline of EMILY's List? Or did the organization's unique structure insulate it from damage?

SUMMARY

There can be little doubt that EMILY's List has undergone a series of organizational transformations over the past twenty years. Understanding how it evolved from a donor network of twenty-five women to a multipronged women's influence organization with over 100,000 members and millions of dollars in annual receipts is an important endeavor.

The organization's success is intimately linked to the political success of women and their power in the U.S. Congress, and its evolution allows us to test and expand several important theories about interest groups. The conventional wisdom concerning interest-group formation has at its core an elite group of politically savvy individuals running the show. That is certainly the case in EMILY'S List, but here is where the similarities end. Whereas other organizations have started as a small group and then spread outward to the grassroots, creating a nonprofit membership organization and/or a nonprofit foundation with an affiliated PAC, EMILY'S List has taken a different path. It has *retained* its status as a PAC and broadened its membership while functioning as a PAC, an interest group, a party adjunct, and a campaign organization. Studying EMILY's List and its origins, structure, strategy, and success, provides a new, more modern understanding of organized interests in American politics *and* women's quest for power. Evidence provided in the chapters that follow will quiet the voices that characterize the organization as simply a women's PAC or a plaything of a few elite women. Rather, EMILY's List is a vibrant, dynamic, broad-based organization with agile leadership and an identity-driven vision that is changing the face of American politics.

The focus of this book is the transformation of the organization from its birthplace in Ellen Malcolm's basement in 1985 to its entrée into presidential politics twenty-four years later. As with any examination of a group or phenomenon that still exists, this book will necessarily leave some wanting more, as some will say that there is no way to understand EMILY's List until after the 2010 election cycle. But there is always another election on the horizon. Given the organization's importance and the relatively scarce systematic examination it has received from academia, this book is much needed. This is not meant to stand as the last word on EMILY's List but rather as the start of a larger conversation about organizational change and the election of women in American politics.

ENDNOTES

1. Political consultant Jeri Rasmussen described EMILY'S List as "the ultimate Tupperware party, with the grand prize being the U.S. Senate seat" (Burrell 1994: 124).
2. Bundling. *The Center for Responsive Politics.* http://www.opensecrets.org/pubs/law_bagtricks/loop5.asp.
3. The organization did not employ professional lobbyists, but rather Malcolm and others gave testimony in congressional hearings on campaign finance legislation and ELIST and its activity is cited in many congressional debates over such legislation.
4. The first known citation for this phrase is Carol Hanisch's essay, "The Personal Is Political," *Feminist Revolution* (1969, 204–205).
5. EMILY's List. 2009. *Where we come from.* http://emilyslist.org/about/where_we_come_from/ (accessed October 17, 2009).
6. Of the 79 women currently serving in the House, only Marcy Kaptur (OH-9) and Kathy Dahlkemper (PA-3) have not received any money from EMILY's List at any point, according to data from the FEC (Center for American Women and Politics 2009b).

Chapter 2

The Second Wave and EMILY's List

As the story goes, Malcolm and twenty-five women met in the basement of Malcolm's Washington, D.C., home one day in 1985, Rolodexes in hand, to embark on a letter-writing campaign (EMILY's List 2009). While a basement might not seem like an auspicious setting to begin a political organization, in many ways it was the perfect location. EMILY's List was borne of frustration and fraternization, most of which can be traced to the Founding Mothers' experience in the women's movement and various political organizations.

One of the most lasting images of the liberal feminist women's movement, beside the protest at the 1968 Miss America pageant, is that of women coming together in consciousness-raising meetings. As Jo Freeman (1975) discussed, these meetings played a key role in the creation of the liberal women's movement, as they fostered a sense of collective experience. The meeting in Malcolm's basement and the pseudo Tupperware parties that followed relied on this memory/tradition of grassroots activity.

The second component of ELIST's founding is funds. Malcolm had the money necessary to cover the organization's startup costs because of her status as the heiress to the IBM fortune.[1] The form of the organization, a political action committee (PAC), was also familiar. After the passage of the Federal Election Campaign Act (FECA) in 1971, the number of PACs exploded well beyond the confines of labor and business, which had dominated the political money game up until that point. Since 1971, in fact, two women's PACs had formed: the National Women's Political Caucus (NWPC) and the Women's Campaign Fund (WCF).

The goal of this chapter is twofold. First, I place EMILY's List in the larger political world of electoral politics and campaign finance. Why did Malcolm create a PAC when there were other women's PACs? What unique tools did PACs offer? Second, I provide a basic history of the organization, focusing on how EMILY's List came into being and its early structure, taking special note of how its structure differed from other women's PACs at the time.

WHY A PAC?

Political action committees (PACs) came into existence in the early 1900s and were most often associated with labor or business interests (Souraf 1994; Sabato 1984). Some scholars (Schattschneider 1975) noted their existence with concern, citing James Madison's warnings regarding the divisiveness of factions or discussing them in reference to corruption or graft. But for the most part, the strength of the political parties limited PAC influence. By the mid-sixties, however, party strength declined and interest groups blossomed, fed in part by the institutionalization of social movements (Ornstein and Elder 1978).

One of the key things many of these groups did was to lobby the government. The effectiveness of lobbying efforts varied; what the group could offer politicians often determined the success of the movement. For instance, groups affiliated with the liberal women's movement or civil rights movement offered government officials a much-needed constituency (Costain 1992, 14), whereas other organizations such as business interests and unions, gained access and influence because of their deep pockets. When campaigns became candidate-centered and campaign consultants became a separate entity, "the burden of raising campaign money passed from party to candidate and the fat cats became as important to candidates as they had been for the parties" (Souraf 1992, 3).

The skyrocketing costs of campaigns—from $200 million in 1964 to $425 million in 1972—reignited earlier concerns about special interests and led to the passage of the Federal Election Campaign Act (hereafter, FECA) in 1971.[2] Yet FECA did not stop President Nixon from extorting upward of $30 million from corporate executives during the 1972 presidential campaign (Sabato 1984, 5). In response, starting in 1974, Congress passed a series of amendments to FECA to stem the tide of money involved in campaigns and elections. These amendments largely focused on limiting the contributions of wealthy individuals, or "fat cats," whom most considered the major problem in the system (Souraf 1992, 9).[3] Not only did the 1974 amendments fail to stop the flow of money into electoral politics, but the newly amended law "...ignored or overlooked the two emerging developments that would push reform off course," namely candidate spending and PACs (Souraf 1992, 11–12).

FECA provided a *legal* framework for interest groups to push their money into the political arena, thereby institutionalizing their existence. Though not mentioned explicitly in FECA, the law established clear rules for political action committees that sought to influence elections through financial contributions. PACs were barred from giving contributions (direct and in-kind) of more than $5,000 a year to a candidate or his or her committee, no more than $15,000 a year to the national parties, and no more than $5,000 a year to any other PAC.[4] In addition to these monies, PACs had the ability to spend an unlimited amount of money on independent expenditures for or against candidates, as long as this spending was "not made in concert or cooperation with or at the request or suggestion of such candidate, the candidate's authorized political committee, or their agents, or a political party committee or its agents."[5]

The 1974 amendments to FECA "guaranteed a place for PACs because their limit [to candidates] was five times that of an individual donor...[making them] the natural and legitimate vehicle for financial participation in campaigns by a wide array of American interest groups" (Sabato 1984, 9–10). Motivated to form PACs by the larger contribution limitations, by the chance for greater participation by members, or even at the "encouragement" of elected officials, the number of registered PACs grew from 722 in 1975 to 3,992 in 1985 and continued to rise.[6]

Souraf (1992) claimed that Federal Election Commission categorization of PACs, "...which began as categories growing out of regulatory imperatives have, surprisingly, become useful analytical categories, because from their legal and structural differences the various kinds of PACs have developed important organizational and behavioral differences" (102). Although all PACs "represent an effort through the accumulation of economic power to influence the outcome of elections, to establish favorable relations with elected officials, or to do both," there are three criteria that differentiate them (Thomas 1978, 82). First, PACs are different than candidate or party committees; they have different contribution limits and filing requirements. Second, PACs are classified into one of six categories: corporate, labor, trade/membership/health, non-connected, cooperative, or corporation without stock.[7] Lastly, and most importantly, PACs are categorized according to whether or not they have a parent organization.

The vast majority of PACs are connected organizations that have a "parent" organization that absorbs the administrative costs of the PAC. All corporate, labor, and trade/membership organizations are considered connected and their PACs are considered separate segregated funds (SSF) by the Federal Election Commission (hereafter, the FEC), the agency created to monitor campaign finance disclosure.[8] There are costs and benefits to being a connected PAC. For example, a SSF can only solicit funds from individuals associated with the parent organization, not the general public.[9] But the limit on solicitations does not keep connected PACs from acquiring donations; as a group, connected PACs have always brought in significantly more receipts than non-connected PACs.

In addition to higher gross receipts, connected PACs enjoy several other important advantages. Since connected PACs do not have the burden of massive overhead costs (which are picked up by the parent organization), they are usually able to give more money to more candidates than their non-connected counterparts. This monetary advantage also allows SSFs to engage in more electoral activities (independent expenditures, GOTV, etc.) to spend more money on lobbyists.

The ability of SSFs to maximize these advantages, however, is dependent on the financial situation of the parent organization.

For example, in 2008, the NFIB PAC (the SSF of the National Federation of Independent Business), acquired receipts of $2,718,621 from over 2,000 donors.[10] That same year, NOW/PAC (the SSF of the National Organization of Women) brought in $252,008 in receipts from 132 individuals, even though the organization has over 500,000 contributing members.[11] Although both of these PACs are connected and have a parent organization that covers their overhead costs, clearly the NFIB PAC is in a better position to capitalize on the other advantages associated with being a connected PAC. Thus, the formal structure of the PAC *can* be an advantage but does not guarantee a PAC's success or failure.

Knowledge of the advantages connected PACs enjoy makes the history of women's PACs and the story of EMILY's List even more intriguing. Within six years, EMILY's List, a non-connected PAC, catapulted itself to the top, becoming *the premier women's PAC*. Souraf (1992) cast the organization as a member of a new class of ideological non-connected PACs:

> ...that go beyond the stereotypical PAC. EMILY's List, for example, is registered as a PAC and makes contributions in the usual ways, but in its pursuit of its feminist agenda it is also a donor network in which membership requires dues of $100 per election and a pledge to contribute at least $100 to at least two candidates endorsed by EMILY's List. It is an organizational form that suits especially the autonomous, politicized contribution, and it may well be a PAC variant with a future. (111)

ELIST achieved this notoriety against the odds. Before explaining its transformation from a donor network, to the premier women's PAC, to a multipronged influence organization, one must first understand the history of women's PACs and their role in electoral politics.

Women's PACs

The first women's PAC, the National Women's Political Caucus (NWPC), formed in 1971 as a membership organization. Its mission was fourfold: increasing the representation of women in politics, recruiting women to run, providing them with campaign funds, and pressuring the political parties to support these female candidates (Salvin 1995, 445). At its inception, NWPC had a small but influential membership: 300 women, including Shirley Chisholm (D-NY) and Bella Abzug (D-NY) and the leaders of various women's groups. By 1975 the organization had grown to more than 30,000 members (Salvin 1995, 445).

While NWPC may have been the first, it was the Women's Campaign Fund (WCF) that became the PAC to beat (Salvin 1995). Created in 1974, the WCF and NWPC were similar in many ways. Both had been formed by a small group of elite female politicos, both stood as connected PACs, and both were bipartisan and focused on electing women to office. The main difference between the two was the nature of their connected status: the parent organization of the WCF was a nonprofit foundation, not a membership organization.[12]

Why is this such a critical difference? Throughout the 1970s, debates raged within women's membership organizations over engagement with the formal political system (Barakso 2005, 64). According to Freeman (1975), the debate was between "woodwork" feminists who were much more comfortable with lobbying and traditional politics versus more radical activists who felt that the only way to affect change was to upend the current institutional arrangements and power structures. The former group recognized that institutional change needed to occur but felt that the best way to accomplish it was through persuasion and piecemeal change. In addition, there were debates within the NWPC over which candidates to support. When Shirley Chisholm, one of the *founding members* of NWPC, ran for President in 1978, the organization did not endorse her until McGovern and McCarthy "proved unworthy of feminist support" (Giddings 1984, 338). In contrast the WCF was connected to a foundation governed by an executive director and a board of trustees. While this still could cause debate over endorsements, the pool of voices was much smaller and the WCF did not have to get membership feedback or approval on decisions. Not coincidentally, the WCF quickly outpaced the NWPC. By 1978 it was the largest and most powerful women's PAC in terms of receipts.

These women's PACs remained small but important players in electoral politics throughout the late 1970s and early 1980s. By the late 1970s, more and more progressive women became engaged in politics at the mass level (the gender gap in voting disappeared in 1980), but at the elite level, women still comprised a small portion of the candidate pool, even with progressive women's PACs there to help.[13] Table 2.1 shows the receipts and candidate contributions for NWPC and WCF from 1980 to 1984, the election before the formation of EMILY's List. The NWPC acquired the least receipts during this period, whereas the WCF consistently received the greatest amount of receipts. Data on the percent of receipts given to candidates is most surprising. From 1980 through 1984, the NWPC and WCF spent less than 50 percent of their respective receipts on candidate contributions, much less than one would expect from connected PACs.[14]

The receipts of the women's PACs were only part of the problem female candidates faced. The cap on PAC donations (FECA mandated that a PAC could only give a candidate $5,000 per election), combined with the high cost of campaigning—in 1982 the average Senate race cost $1.78 million—meant that candidates had to obtain considerable funding from individuals, from

TABLE 2.1. Receipts and candidate contributions by select women's PACs, 1980–1984.

Year	NWPC-CSC and Victory Fund			Women's Campaign Fund/Forum PAC[1]		
	Receipts	$ to Candidates	% Contributions to Receipts	Receipts	$ to Candidates	% Contributions to Receipts
1980	$31,677	$11,500	36.3%	$459,830	$72,763	15.8%
1982	$14,080	$4,300	30.5%	$593,099	$53,975	9.1%
1984	$71,750	$30,500	42.5%	$957,642	$128,200	13.4%

Source. Data from the Federal Election Commission.
Note. [1]The Women's Campaign Fund became the Women's Campaign Forum, a non-profit 501(c)(4) with an affiliated PAC (WCF-PAC) and a sister organization, the Women's Campaign Forum Foundation, in 2004. Personal communication with Ilana Goldman, April 2008. See also www.wcf.org.

other PACs, or from the parties in order to run a viable competitive campaign (Ornstein, Mann, and Malbin 2008). Acquiring these other types of donations posed problems, as the high rate of incumbency and the persistent gap in women's elected status dictated that most female candidates were challengers (Burrell 1994).

A challenger typically receives far less money from PACs and interest groups than an incumbent. The roots of this discrepancy lie in the access strategy used by PACs—that is, PACs give money to legislators to gain access in the hopes that access will lead to influence (Magee 2002). Although scholars have not been able to prove influence—that is, they have not been able to find a direct correlation between interest-group money and roll-call votes—they have found that the access PACs gain through campaign contributions influences committee outcomes and the wording of legislation. (Magee 2002; Smith 1995).

This access strategy might have been beneficial to PACs, but it had negative consequences for most female candidates. Since female candidates typically ran as challengers, they were denied funding by access-oriented PACs and therefore rarely received enough money to run a viable campaign. Consequently, although women's PACs formed to benefit women, in the 1970s and early 1980s, they had limited success in meeting their main goal: electing women to public office.

Those women who managed to make it into public office were often viewed as "token" members. However, that began to change in the mid-1970s. Gertzog (1995) found that the women who ran for public office after 1970 tended to be "experienced, highly motivated, career public servants who carefully calculate the personal and political benefits of running for higher office, assess the probability of their winning, and determine the personal and political costs of defeat ..." (4). By the late 1970s, women were

"...shedding the delicacy and aloofness that had precluded them from acting as decision makers and accepting instead a gloves-off approach to the culture and the trade-offs of the political marketplace" (Tolchin and Tolchin 1974, 27). The emergence of a new type of female candidate is linked to women's experience in the liberal women's movement. Movement politics had taught them about power—both its sources and its limits.

The introduction of a different type of female legislator in the late 1970s corresponds to a larger societal change, most notably an increased number of women obtaining graduate and professional degrees. As women began entering fields such as history, political science, and sociology, an increasing number turned their attention to understanding the role and place of women within each of these disciplines. By the mid-to-late 1970s, female scholars began asking questions about women's political participation, using the tools of their disciplines to find the answers and using the answers to inform their activism.[15]

While more women were going to college and entering the workforce than ever before, women were not acquiring wealth at the same rate as men. The gender gap in wages and the rise in the number of female-headed households meant that women had less disposable income. Thus, the irony of women's PACs at this time meant that those women who needed better representation in Congress most were unable to give money to the organizations that could help make those changes happen. Furthermore, running for political office was not something that the majority of women were willing or able to consider.

That began to change in the early 1980s. The gender gap in *voting turnout* disappeared in the 1980 presidential election, but a gender gap in *vote choice* emerged.[16] The 1980 presidential election also brought the first anti-ERA, pro-life President into the Oval Office. The neo-conservative movement that began with

Goldwater in 1968 finally had a voice in the White House and gained control of the Republican Party, much to the dismay of liberal women's organizations. That, combined with the failure to ratify the Equal Rights Amendment (ERA) in 1982—which had served as a rallying point for the liberal feminist women's movement since its passage in 1972—left "groups within the women's movement in a state of disarray" on two fronts (Costain 1992, 120).

Internally, the two threads of the movement argued amongst themselves over future strategy, finances, and leadership (Barakso 2005, 90–92); externally the movement's very public failure precipitated its loss of influence in national politics. The number of pro-woman pieces of legislation and court decisions continually declined throughout the Reagan administration. Whereas in the 1970s, 72.7 percent of judicial and legislative outcomes were favorable to the women's movement, during the Reagan administration, the percentage of favorable court decisions dropped to 50 percent, reaching a nadir of 14.3 percent during George H. Bush's presidency (Bashevkin 1994, 681–685). Activists saw the period of 1980–1992 as one that brought "racism and social division…fear of the new Right…and policy rollback(s)" (Bashevkin 1994, 692).

In retrospect, good things came out of this tumultuous time. "Feminist groups altered their focus and tried to build on changes in public consciousness that were beyond the control of presidential administrations," which brought "more momentum and more public support…[awareness] of the obvious enemy…and a financial and mobilization bonanza for many women's organizations…" (Bashevkin 1994, 692; Taylor 1989).

More importantly for women and electoral politics, the liberal feminist movement blamed the failure of the ERA on sexist male legislators. Only thirty-four women held state-level elected office in 1982; they comprised 10.5 percent of all elected state-level offices.[17] Women made up an even smaller percentage of officeholders at the national level. Twenty-three women served in the 97th Congress (1981–1983): twenty-one in the House and two in the Senate. Together, they comprised 4 percent of the membership in Congress. Women's groups used the failure of the ERA as a call to arms, claiming that the only way to protect and promote progressive women's issues was to increase the number of women in public office (Mansbridge 1986). That call did not go unanswered. According to data from the Center for American Women and Politics, between 1970 and 1984, an average of fifty women ran for U.S. Congress each cycle; in 1984 seventy-five women ran for public office, up 29 percent from 1980.[18]

Women's PACs were not ready for the influx of female candidates in 1984. Even though they benefitted from their status as SSFs, as mentioned previously, these organizations were constrained in terms of how much financial support they could provide candidates. Female candidates needed the money women's PACs *could* provide, but $30,000 (if all three women's PACs gave the maximum amount in the primary and general election) was inadequate to cover the costs of a viable campaign. They needed the money from parties, other PACs, and individuals. But these contributions would only come if the candidate could prove herself, which involved more than filing papers.

Proving one's viability required a multifaceted approach. The candidate and her campaign team had to understand polling, campaign ads, and so on. Women's PACs knew what it meant to run a viable campaign; that's why recruiting and training women to run for office were part of their mission. But up until this point, women's PACs were unable to build an effective recruitment and training program with enough viable women in the pipeline because of the sporadic nature of the candidate pool and the larger apathy of female voters. This situation, however, changed when the failure of the ERA showed mass-level women the need for descriptive representation.

THE BIRTH OF EMILY'S LIST

The frustration that brought the Founding Mothers together in Ellen Malcolm's basement in 1985 was the direct result of the events of the preceding decade. Malcolm had been active in the women's movement and electoral politics for over a decade, working first at Common Cause and the National Women's Political Caucus in the early to mid-1970s, and then as press secretary to Esther Peterson, special adviser to President Jimmy Carter.[19] Upon graduation from the MBA program at George Washington University, Malcolm created the Windom Fund and began using her IBM fortune to surreptitiously fund female candidates (Clift and Brazaitas 2003, 30). She knew that female candidates needed money; she also knew that there was a dearth of women in the candidate pool.

When Harriet Woods decided to run for a seat in the U.S. Senate in 1982, Malcolm joined her campaign staff. Woods was a viable female Democratic candidate running for the U.S. Senate, and she lost, by all accounts, because she ran out of money in the last days of the election (Woods 2001). This situation, coupled with the loss of the ERA battle earlier in the year, left Malcolm and many of her Democratic friends and colleagues frustrated but resolute. Malcolm believed that if Woods and other women like her had enough "early" money to make them competitive in the primaries (the average total cost of a House or Senate race in 1984 was $241,000 and $2.3 million respectively), women could and would win (Ornstein, Mann, and

Malbin 2001–2002, 87–93). Lael Stegall, a friend who helped Malcolm establish and run the Windom Fund, advised Malcolm to stop using her money indirectly. At Stegall's encouragement, Malcolm decided to create a PAC and reached out to her friends for help. Malcolm's friends shared her frustration with the direction of the country and the continued inequality women faced. Together, they possessed the money, motive, and moxie that Malcolm knew were needed to create an organization that would have real influence.

THE EMILY'S LIST MODEL

Malcolm knew that her fortune and the bank accounts of her friends would not sustain the organization, and ELIST did not have a parent organization to bear costs, so Malcolm created EMILY's List in a slow strategic way. Instead of using direct mail—a relatively new and costly endeavor (Sabato 1981)— Malcolm built ELIST on the back of a preexisting social network. When discussing the organization, she did not characterize it as a PAC but as a donor network.

This decision paid off in multiple ways. First, to some degree this took the pressure off Malcolm in terms of expectations for the organization. Since the organization was marketed as a donor network, if recommended candidates lost, it could be blamed on a lack of donations because of the continued economic gap between men and women. Second, a donor network implied some measure of donor control, although ELIST was consciously crafted as a hierarchical organization in which decisions were made by Malcolm and the organization staff. Aware of the problems some women's organizations faced because of their democratic decision-making structure, Malcolm did not want ELIST to suffer the same fate. This would be especially important in the early days of the organization, before its "track record" had been established. Thus, Malcolm marketed EMILY's list as an investment—an investment in a candidate, in an organization, and in a future where women had an equal voice on the floor of the U.S. Congress.

Key to the effectiveness of EMILY's List as a donor network was bundling, which Malcolm had raised "to an art form" (Day and Hadley 2005, 6). Bundlers, or brokers, have played a role in moneyed politics since at least the nineteenth century. These individuals have served as the conduit between the political parties and the "fat cats" who provide the parties with funds.

> The brokers of today are the descendants of the fat cats, the old party treasurers, the campaign managers, and the finance committees and their chairpeople who raised the money in the old days. And just as then, they bring a third set of interest to the contributor-candidate exchanges. (Souraf 1992, 129)

When the parties' influence declined in the mid-twentieth century, the influence of brokers increased, as these individuals knew how to help candidates raise the funds necessary to buy precious television time and the services of political consultants.

Malcolm's decision to bundle was not revolutionary. The decision by PACs to bundle money seems like a no-brainer—it is simply one more way that a PAC can gain influence with a candidate. However, the decision to bundle is not a popular one, according to Sabato (1984), because of one major risk. Donors *could* submit a bundled check addressed to a candidate not endorsed by the organization, leaving the organization with no choice but to transmit the money to the candidate, thus endorsing the candidate by default. The chance this will happen keeps many PACs from bundling.

However, the benefits that bundling can bring to an organization often outweigh the costs (Thomas 1978, 84–86); that is certainly the case for ELIST. Bundling often does more for the bundler than for the recipient *or* the donor.

> The variety of cases, the configuration of interests, the enhancement of political goals—the possibilities are virtually endless in the universe of brokered contributions. By all informal accounts and alarms, the role of the broker grows with each passing electoral cycle....The brokers' interests are those of the contributor writ large, and their many brokerings make themselves into an influential elite that some have called the new fat cats of American campaign finance. (Souraf 1992, 125–126)

Just how much bundling did Malcolm accomplish? EMILY's List has consistently increased its bundling activity over time; in fact, the money that EMILY's List bundles to candidates *far* outpaces the amount of money the organization gives to candidates in direct or in-kind contributions. Receiving bundled funds from EMILY's List is an elite honor; only 24 of the 115 female Democratic women running for Congress in 2000 received a bundled contribution from an EMILY'S List member. That number declined in 2002 and 2004 but significantly increased in 2006, when 38 of 157 female Democratic candidates received bundled funds through EMILY's List.

A comparison of candidate contributions from ELIST with candidate contributions from other women's PACs (table 2.2) shows that, as expected from a non-connected PAC, ELIST has never give more than 20 percent of its receipts to candidates in direct or in-direct contributions. The other women's PACs, benefitting from their connected PAC status, have traditionally given a larger percentage of their receipts to candidates. From this, one would imagine that these other women's PACs are more active,

TABLE 2.2. Receipts and candidate contributions from EMILY's List and select women's PACs, 1986–2008.

Year	NWPC-CSC and Victory Fund Receipts	$ to Candidates	% Contributions to Receipt	Women's Campaign Fund/Forum PAC Receipts	$ to Candidates	% Contributions to Receipt	EMILY's List Receipts	$ to Candidates	% Contributions to Receipt
1986	$54,192	$8,150	15.0%	$1,087,503	$106,956	9.8%	$212,324	$27,510	13.0%
1988	$56,705	$28,155	49.7%	$1,119,595	$123,012	11.0%	$417,922	$70,647	16.9%
1990	$31,268	$7,750	24.8%	$1,143,732	$125,355	11.0%	$973,124	$71,013	7.3%
1992	$76,205	$69,800	91.6%	$1,980,430	$519,567	26.2%	$4,425,157	$348,007	7.9%
1994	$58,007	$35,750	61.6%	$1,815,052	$262,338	14.5%	$7,422,835	$227,689	3.1%
1996	$18,855	$16,500	87.5%	$2,778,428	$307,185	11.1%	$13,619,906	$253,218	1.9%
1998	$27,465	$26,200	95.4%	$2,405,553	$148,643	6.2%	$14,237,394	$238,721	1.7%
2000	$20,438	$16,150	79.0%	$1,541,565	$74,294	4.8%	$21,201,339	$221,746	1.0%
2002	$9,403	$7,900	84.0%	$1,713,677	$87,400	5.1%	$22,682,406	$202,975	0.9%
2004	$13,363	$6,000	44.9%	$1,781,884	$86,482	4.9%	$34,128,818	$120,535	0.4%
2006	$5,307	$6,200	116.8%	$921,268	$59,517	6.5%	$34,118,930	$278,436	0.8%
2008	$19,721	$16,750	84.9%	$223,335	$118,478	53.0%	$35,232,112	$244,951	0.7%

Source. Data from the Federal Election Commission.

TABLE 2.3. Candidate contributions (including bundled money) from EMILY's List and select women's PACs, 1986–2008.

Year	NWPC $ to Candidates	WCF $ to Candidates	ELIST $ to Candidates
1986	$8,150	$106,956	$14,807
1988	$28,155	$123,012	$134,662
1990	$7,750	$125,355	$269,588
1992	$69,800	$519,567	$1,234,500
1994	$35,750	$262,338	$1,049,704
1996	$16,500	$307,185	$1,629,058
1998	$26,200	$148,643	$1,973,277
2000	$16,150	$74,294	$2,812,776
2002	$7,900	$87,400	$6,401,144
2004	$6,000	$86,482	$8,445,317
2006	$6,200	$59,517	$8,517,875
2008	$16,750	$118,478	$6,024,320

Source. Data from Federal Election Commission and Political Moneyline.

but again the raw data show us otherwise. The NWPC and WCF gave much less money to candidates overall, especially after the 1996 election. If bundled money is added to the total given to candidates (see table 2.3), it becomes clear how bundling has set ELIST apart from these other women's PACs.

THE "DEMOCRATIC QUEENMAKER"

Bundling made Malcolm into *the* broker for female Democratic pro-choice candidates. She became "the queen of the hat-passers"—the "democratic queenmaker"—and a power broker within the Democratic Party (Spake 1988). This partisan component of the EMILY's List model is the second way Malcolm consciously crafted EMILY's List to be different from the other women's PACs. In many ways, it is this relationship that helped her propel EMILY's List into the top tier of moneyed politics.

As discussed earlier, many in the liberal women's movement advocated a bipartisan approach, believing that it provided them with the best chances for success (Costain 1992; Barakso 2005). The NWPC and WCF were created in that tradition. Harriet Woods, former Senate candidate and president of NWPC from 1991–1995, hesitated to assume the presidency at the bipartisan NWPC because "…[it] meant I'd not only have to give up my institute at the university but also all partisan Democratic activities" (Woods 2001, 136). But Malcolm and the other Founding Mothers saw bipartisanship as one of the reasons that women's PACs remained small and the successes of the women's movement were in jeopardy by the mid-1980s. When asked about the factors that led to the formation of EMILY's List, Founding Mother Joanne Howes stated, "…the National Women's Political Caucus was bipartisan. Most of us were Democrats and we wanted to put our energy and resources in something partisan. [Furthermore] women did not have the kind of support [they needed] from the Democratic National Committee."[20]

It was not so much that the other women's PACs rejected the Democratic Party. In fact, many of the candidates they supported were Democrats, and the NWPC had been instrumental in pressuring the Democratic Party to change the conventional delegate rules to mandate an equal number of male and female delegates (Burrell 2004). But because the organizations were bipartisan, the pressure they could put on the Democratic Party was limited. However, by the mid-1990s, EMILY's List would become a critical resource for the Democratic Party. Again, building on preexisting networks, Malcolm expanded EMILY's List in such a way that it became a party adjunct, giving the Party money, recruiting and vetting candidates, and by 2001, training campaign professionals and volunteers to work on Democratic campaigns.

EMILY's List and the Democratic Party: Part One

In 1992 ELIST exploded in terms of membership and receipts, and the organization began giving money to the Democratic Party. PACs giving money to the parties is not new—in fact, it was seen as a way for individuals and groups to insure influence dating back to the nineteenth century. Souraf pointed to the significant amount of money Labor gave to the Democratic Party in 1988 as part of the explanation for its access and influence in the Democratic Party organization (1992, 110). The relationship between the parties and PACs became deeper in the 1990s as PACs began to give parties soft money donations to use for party building.

Soft money is best understood in contrast to hard money. Hard money donations from individuals and PACs to the parties were regulated by the FEC under FECA. However, until the passage of the Bipartisan Campaign Reform Act (BCRA) in 2002, PACs could give limitless amounts of soft money to the parties as long as that money was used for "party building" activities—such as, "get out the vote" (GOTV) efforts or issue advocacy (Dwyre and Kolodny 2003; see also Federal Election Commission 2002).

In stark contrast to the other women's PACs, starting in 1990, EMILY's List provided the national Democratic Party with some type of monetary contribution (originally soft money, and then after BCRA, hard dollar contributions; see table 2.4.).[21] Not only did EMILY's List give soft money to the national Democratic Party, but since the mid-1990s, it has given soft money to

TABLE 2.4. Money given by women's PACs to national political parties, 1980–2008.

Year	Contributions from Party		Contributions to Party	
	EMILY's List	Other Select Women's PACs*	EMILY's List	Other Select Women's PACs
1980	$-	$-	$-	$-
1982	$-	$-	$-	$-
1984	$-	$-	$-	$-
1986	$-	$-	$-	$-
1988	$-	$-	$-	$-
1990	$5,500	$-	$-	$-
1992	$50	$-	$74,955	$1,500
1994	$3,600	$-	$69,596	$-
1996	$71,732	$-	$230,250	$-
1998	$4,000	$-	$244,888	$-
2000	$60,000	$-	$123,488	$-
2002	$135,835	$-	$155,000	$-
2004	$36,199	$-	$113,030	$1,000
2006	$7,750	$-	$180,852	$-
2008	$4,650	$-	$185,004	$-

Source. Data from the Federal Election Commission.
Note. NWPC, WCF, NOW-PAC.

the Democratic Party in various states—a practice that was not banned with the passage of the Bipartisan Campaign Reform Act.

In 1994 EMILY's List began its own "get out the vote" program: WOMEN VOTE! While the focus of WOMEN VOTE! is to educate voters and increase turnout for endorsed EMILY's List candidates, by its very nature the WOMEN VOTE! program also helps Democratic candidates up and down the ticket. For example, in 2004, EMILY's List flew more than 500 volunteers to Florida the week before the election to canvass neighborhoods, "knocking on 506,000 doors to bring home a victory for progressive values."[22] ELIST also ran a GOTV program in South Carolina that year, placing "171,000 computerized calls...to provide them [Democratic voters] with precinct information" (Reynolds 2004; Russakoff 2004). These activities fostered and strengthened the bonds between EMILY's List and the Democratic Party at both the national and state level (Biersack and Viray 2005, 70; Semiatin and Rozell 2005, 76).[23]

But Malcolm and EMILY's List were not only a money tree for the Party to shake. Through ELIST, Malcolm recruited and vetted viable female candidates to run for office and win. As EMILY's List began to build a record of successful endorsements, the Party began to step up to the plate in terms of supporting candidates endorsed by ELIST. Historically speaking, no party has been given high marks for its recruitment efforts vis-à-vis women, but more recent research indicates that in the past twenty years, the Democratic Party has done a better job recruiting and funding female candidates. The efforts of EMILY's List are key to this change in Party behavior (Burrell 1994; Day and Hadley 2005; Sanbonmatsu 2004).

By the mid-1990s, ELIST's vetting apparatus facilitated its emergence as a "lead" PAC. Lead PACs play a critical role in a candidate's campaign. If a candidate can get the support of a lead PAC, more money and support will follow. For example, an organization, such as COPE or BIPAC, signals to other PACs that a candidate is viable and worthy of support. "If BIPAC contributes to a candidate, its action may well trigger, or at least encourage, contributions to the same candidate from other business PACs. Similarly a candidate who receives support from COPE is virtually assured to some level of funding from other labor PACs" (Biersack and

Viray 2005, 54; Herrnson 2005; Thomas 1978). For female Democratic pro-choice candidates running as challengers, ELIST's status as a lead PAC provided a critical boost to their electoral prospects.

The third way Malcolm crafted ELIST different than other PACs was her pursuit of both descriptive *and* substantive representation vis-à-vis EMILY's List. Whereas the other major women's PACs either focused on descriptive representation (supporting all female candidates regardless of party or issue position) *or* focused on substantive representation (which meant supporting male candidates who took the "right" position on key issues), only female pro-choice, pro-ERA Democratic candidates are eligible for an EMILY's List endorsement.

EMILY's List is concerned with substantive representation (all endorsed candidates have to be pro-choice and pro-ERA), but it does not employ lobbyists.[24] That said, at some level the entire mission of ELIST is a substantive one. ELIST and its membership are all driven to elect more women to political office because of the belief that these women will behavior differently than their male counterparts. However, the substantive component of ELIST's mission is deployed in an atypical fashion. PACs that pursue substantive goals often use the access strategies discussed earlier. They typically focus on electing incumbents. However, Malcolm and the Founding Mothers were not willing to sacrifice their substantive goals or their descriptive goals. To insure that EMILY's List never sacrificed either for expediency's sake, both descriptive and substantive goals were embedded within the organization's endorsement criteria.

Conclusion

In 1985 Malcolm knew that female candidates needed money, but she also knew they needed a politically savvy, well-funded support network. After the defeat of the ERA and the defeat of Harriet Woods, she knew that the existing women's PACs were inadequate. Malcolm used her own fortune and her network of friends to craft EMILY's List in a particular way. First, she marketed EMILY's List as a donor network and used her connections to find women (and a few men) who were upset about the direction of the country and had the money and motivation to do something about it. Second, Malcolm made the organization's endorsement criteria reflect the descriptive and substantive goals of the organization: a woman had to be a viable, pro-choice, pro-ERA Democrat. Third, ELIST was created as a partisan organization and Malcolm quickly made the organization invaluable to the Democratic Party. As a result of these decisions, by 1991 EMILY's List was in a position to take advantage of any political opportunity that came its way.

In the next chapter, I describe the events that took EMILY's List—a mere women's donor network—and transformed it into a multipronged influence organization and a major player in the world of money politics. By 2008, every aspect of the organization's structure and strategy had evolved—only the importance of identity politics and the role of Malcolm as the organization's entrepreneurial leader remained unchanged.

Endnotes

1. According to Spake (1988), Malcolm had hidden her wealth from even her closest friends for years.
2. According to Souraf (1992), this occurred most notably with the Democrats, driven by the ability of the GOP to raise more money.
3. One of the main goals of FECA in 1971 was to establish a public financing system and to place limits on the amount of money candidates could spend in elections. Those limits were struck down by the Supreme Court in *Buckley v. Valeo* (1976).
4. http://www.fec.gov/law/feca/feca.pdf. Federal election campaign laws. 2008. Federal Election Commission. http://www.fec.gov/law/feca/feca.pdf (accessed May 1, 2009).
5. http://www.fec.gov/law/feca/feca.pdf. Federal election campaign laws. 2008. Federal Election Commission. http://www.fec.gov/law/feca/feca.pdf (accessed May 1, 2009).
6. According to Sabato (1984), there are at least five reasons to start a PAC. First, as mentioned previously, PACs have more leeway to give money than individuals, though the amount they are practically able to give depends heavily on whether the PAC has a parent organization that foots the PAC's administrative costs. Second, government has a greater impact on some groups than others. Third, groups will have more influence if members are active in politics—giving money gives members a material stake in elections. Fourth, the creation of a PAC can be the result of external pressure from elected officials. Finally, it may simply be a public relations ploy (29–31).
7. The FEC summary files include a column named SIG. According to the codebook for the summary file, "This indicates the organization with which the committee has reported being connected. In most cases, these sponsoring organizations cannot use treasury funds to directly make political contributions. The law does, however, permit them to pay the overhead costs of these committees." ftp://ftp.fec.gov/FEC/pacsum92.txt. PAC financial summaries (end of cycle). 1992. Federal Election Commission. http://fec.gov/finance/disclosure/ftpsum.shtml (accessed January 5, 2009).

8. http://www.fec.gov/pages/brochures/ssfvnonconnected.shtml. SSFs and nonconnected PACs. 2008. Federal Election Commission. http://www.fec.gov/pages/brochures/ssfvnonconnected.shtml (accessed January 5, 2009).
9. http://www.fec.gov/pdf/colagui.pdf. Federal election commission campaign guide: Corporations and labor organizations. 2007. Federal Election Commission. http://www.fec.gov/pdf/colagui.pdf (accessed January 5, 2009).
10. http://www.opensecrets.org/pacs/pacgave.php?cmte=C00101105&cycle=2008. National Federation of independent business contributors. 2008. Open Secrets: Center for Responsive Politics. http://www.opensecrets.org/pacs/pacgave.php?cmte=C00101105&cycle=2008 (accessed January 5, 2009).
11. http://www.now.org/about.html. About NOW. 2009. National Organization for Women. http://www.now.org/about.html (accessed January 5, 2009).
12. http://www.wcfonline.org/sn/overview. WCF overview. 2009. Women's Campaign Fund. http://www.wcfonline.org/sn/overview (accessed January 5, 2009).
13. http://www.cawp.rutgers.edu/fast_facts/elections/documents/can_histsum.pdf. Summary of women candidates for selected offices 1970–2008: Major party nominees. 2008. Center for American Women and Politics: Fact sheet. http://www.cawp.rutgers.edu/fast_facts/elections/documents/can_histsum.pdf (accessed January 5, 2009).
14. It is important to note that the level of receipts and candidate contributions by NWPC, WCF, and NOW/PAC are miniscule when compared to the activity of AFL-CIO's PAC, COPE, or BIPAC (the Business Industry PAC). See records of the Federal Election Commission at www.fec.gov.
15. Some of the earliest literature on women and politics addresses women as voters and participants at the mass level. See Conway 1985; Freeman 1975; McGlen and O'Connor 1983; Sapiro 1983; and Mueller 1988. This literature largely fits outside the scope of this paper, as I am more concerned with the attention scholars have paid to female candidates and female politicians.
16. http://www.cawp.rutgers.edu/fast_facts/voters/gender_gap.php. Fast facts: Gender gap in voting. 2008. Center for American Women

and Politics. http://www.cawp.rutgers.edu/fast_facts/voters/gender_gap.php (accessed January 5, 2009).
17. Data from the Center of American Woman and Politics. http://www.cawp.rutgers.edu/Facts/Officeholders/cong.pdf . Women in the U.S. Congress 2009. 2009. Center for American Women and Politics. http://www.cawp.rutgers.edu/fast_facts/levels_of_office/documents/cong.pdf (accessed January 5, 2009).
18. http://www.cawp.rutgers.edu/fast_facts/elections/documents/can_histsum.pdf. Summary of women candidates for selected offices 1970–2008: Major party nominees. 2008. Center for American Women and Politics: Fact sheet. http://www.cawp.rutgers.edu/fast_facts/elections/documents/can_histsum.pdf (accessed January 5, 2009).
19. http://emilyslist.org/about/senior_leadership_malcolm/index.html. Senior leadership: Ellen R. Malcolm President and Founder. 2007. Emily's List. http://emilyslist.org/about/senior_leadership_malcolm/index.html (accessed January 5, 2009).
20. Author interview of Joanne Howes on April 15, 2008, in Washington, D.C.
21. http://opensecrets.org/softmoney/softcomp2.asp?txtName=National+Women%27s+Political+Caucus&txtUltOrg=y&txtSort=name&txtCycle=2002; http://opensecrets.org/softmoney/softcomp1.asp?txtName=EMILY%27s+List (accessed January 10, 2009).
22. See: http://www.emilyslist.org/gallery/FLGOTV, http://www.emilyslist.org/team_emily/wcaarchive/folakeoguntebi.html and http://www.emilyslist.org/team_emily/wcaarchive/pepecervantes.html (accessed March 1, 2006).
23. Beirsack and Viray found that the NRA, COPE, and the NAACP have "focused much of their electoral efforts on voter mobilization and communications targeting their large membership" since the late 1990s (Biersack and Viray 2005, 70). Semiatan and Rozell (2005) pointed out that from 1996 to 2000, PAC "get out the vote" (GOTV) strategies changed from a focus on television advertising to television ads supplemented by registration drives, phone banks, and direct mail (80).
24. "PAC for women expects no monetary payback" (*The Houston Chronicle* 1992).

CHAPTER 3

THE TRANSFORMATION OF EMILY'S LIST

Chapter 2 discussed the basic differences between political action committees (PACs) and how those differences can affect an organization's success. In particular, certain political opportunities—namely the passage of FECA in 1971, the election of Ronald Reagan in 1980, and the failure of the ERA in 1982—all provided women and women's PACs with opportunities.

In some ways, the resources and skills female candidates needed to win were understood by the women's PACs that emerged in the 1970s. The mission statements of the National Women's Political Caucus (NWPC) and the Women's Campaign Fund (WCF) included recruiting female candidates and supporting and protecting feminist policies as part of their goals. However, these organizations suffered from several limitations that Malcolm consciously avoided when she and the Founding Mothers formed EMILY's List. These decisions—to start a nonconnected PAC but market it as a donor network based on a preexisting social network, to link substantive goals (pro-choice and pro-ERA) to descriptive goals (the desire for more women in public office), and lastly, to be a partisan organization and provide various types of support and services to the Democratic Party—paid off. Over the next twenty years, EMILY's List expanded dramatically, beginning several new projects, reorganizing and expanding its structure to include several new divisions, becoming deeply connected to the Democratic Party as well as other PACs, and reaching out to new members.

In the 1986 and 1990 elections combined, ten out of twenty-five pro-choice, pro-ERA female Democratic candidates endorsed by EMILY's List were elected to the U.S. Congress; all of these women cited EMILY's List as critical to their victory.[1] But these wins only increased female representation in Congress to 6 percent by 1990, and the protection of a woman's right to choose continued to erode (Center for American Women in Politics 2009a; Benson Gold 1980; Robertson 1992). As was the case with the emergence of ELIST in 1985, in 1992 the organization again benefited from the convergence of political opportunity and resource mobilization. Ten years later, EMILY's List became a full-service political organization, and by 2008, it stood as the exemplar of a new model of political organization.

HILL-THOMAS CONTROVERSY AND THE 1992 ELECTION

In October 1991, Anita Hill claimed that Clarence Thomas, nominee for the United States Supreme Court, sexually harassed her when he served as her supervisor (*CNN Special Report* 2005).

Hill's allegations, and the controversy that ensued, became a lightning rod for women and women's groups who were outraged at Thomas's alleged behavior but just as outraged at the behavior of the all-male Senate Judiciary committee in charge of Thomas' confirmation hearings. Women's groups and women's PACs, especially ELIST, capitalized on women's outrage; reminiscent of 1982, they called for women to run for office. The NWPC took out a full-page ad in the *New York Times* portraying the Senate hearings as a farce (Burrell 2004, 36). Ellen Malcolm was interviewed by *60 Minutes* and various other national news outlets (Burrell 2004, 148).

The media began to describe Malcolm as the "fairy godmother to feminist politicians" (Grogan 1992). Memberships and money streamed into ELIST's Washington, D.C., office. An unprecedented 119 women ran for Congress that year and 2,396 women ran for state-level office.[2] Twenty-four ELIST-endorsed candidates—all female, pro-choice, pro-ERA Democrats—were elected in November 1992 (EMILY's List 2009). By the end of 1992, ELIST boasted 23,000 members and received more than $4.4 million in receipts. The organization supplied $348,007 in contributions to candidates and bundled another $5.8 million to endorsed candidates (EMILY's List 2009).[3] The organization's success in getting money to its candidates and having its candidates elected propelled EMILY's List into the national spotlight.

Malcolm was not satisfied with ELIST's new favored status. Prior experience told her that one year of receipts and high membership numbers would not be enough to create an organization strong enough to withstand the bad years (partisan shifts, losses, lower receipts, fewer candidates, etc.). After all, the WCF had been heralded as *the* premier women's PAC just one cycle earlier. Furthermore, Malcolm's experience in the NWPC and on Woods' campaign showed her that women did not just need money; female candidates who had money could lose. To be competitive and remain competitive, female candidates needed to be trained on how to become and/or how to remain viable. They needed access to trained campaign professionals who understood polling, campaign advertisements, and "get out the vote" (GOTV) efforts. They needed support from other PACs and the Democratic Party. Finally, they needed the outraged women of 1991 to continue to send them money and then to show up at the voting booth and cast their ballot on Election Day.

THE 1992 ELECTION AND THE FOUR CORNERSTONES

As previously mentioned, a record number of women ran for federal and state office in 1992: up 52 percent and 11 percent (respectively) over 1990 figures.[4] While many heralded the successes of 1992, dubbing it the "Year of the Woman," Malcolm did not let EMILY's List rest on its laurels. Political strategists knew that the success of women in the 1992 election was in part due to the high number of open seats, which female candidates, if adequately funded, had as good a chance at winning as their male counterparts (Burrell 1994). Furthermore, the political context of the election—i.e., the general anti-incumbent political atmosphere and the emphasis on domestic affairs, on which female candidates are typically viewed as more credible by voters—also facilitated these gains (Carroll 1994). In the election postmortem, it became clear that several external factors (other than incumbency and ambition) were critical to a female candidate's success; in 1992, these were credibility, money, mobilization, and the media (Witt, Matthews and Paget 1994).

These are factors that ELIST tried to control in its earlier endorsement choices by endorsing individuals that Malcolm and the Founding Mothers knew well and by focusing membership drives on mobilizing preexisting networks. But future success would require a more extensive effort. It is not a coincidence that the "four cornerstones" discussed by Witt, Matthews, and Paget (1994) are the very factors that EMILY's List focused on for its future agenda. Before discussing how these factors became the foundation of a new model of political organization, it is important to have a basic understanding of the distinctive impact these four factors have on female campaigns.

The First Cornerstone: Media and Campaigns

The media and campaigns are critical to a candidate's electoral prospects, as both provide cues and information that become the basis of every voter's decision-making process. Given the role of the media and campaigns in our democratic system, gender differences in media coverage or in campaign style and presentation are a cause for great concern. Scholars have found that different aspects of the media can have a different impact on female candidates than male candidates.

First, the media can perpetuate stereotypes about female and male candidates in the questions reporters ask and the type of stories the media tells about candidates (Kahn 1996). For example, news organizations may run stories on a female candidate's clothing choices or the impact of campaigning on a female candidate's family—two topics rarely discussed in coverage of male candidates. This, in turn, may prime voters to: 1) focus on a female candidate's physical features rather than on her issue positions or ideas; and/or 2) focus on a female candidate's family life. Stories about a female candidate's family life, especially who is caring for her children and the division of labor within her household, can prime a voter to evaluate a female candidate as a mother or a wife. If a voter believes that women should adhere to more traditional roles such as childrearing, especially when children are younger, this type of coverage could significantly affect an individual's vote choice.

Female candidates sometimes fall prey to gender stereotypes themselves, which can affect how they present themselves and their campaign style (Fox 1997). These gender differences in campaign style and media coverage, as well as voter and candidate stereotypes, make access to a well-trained campaign staff critically important. Women typically have smaller and less professional campaign organizations (Fox 1997, 28). Brewer (2005) found that women's underrepresentation in the field of political consulting was the result of several factors, including family demands, business climate, sexist clients, and early career decisions such as a lack of campaign experience (154–158). She argued, and Kornacki (2006) concurred, that the presence of female consultants on campaigns is critically important because "women might lend a fresh approach...they may be more collaborative...[and] women campaign managers might be better at advising men how to present themselves to women voters" (41).

THE SECOND CORNERSTONE: CREDIBILITY

Credibility can be an issue for some female candidates, particularly those who have never held political office. Witt, Matthews, and Paget (1994) found that voters rated female candidates as more "trustworthy" than their male counterparts. In 1992 stereotypes about female candidates' credibility on domestic policy issues may have helped some candidates, as domestic policy dominated that election (Abramowitz 1995). However, the saliency or importance of domestic concerns in a voter's mind is not constant; in the 2002 midterm elections, foreign policy dominated voters' minds (Jacobson 2003).

In order to succeed, female candidates must have the "right experience" in the eyes of voters; they must also be aware of the potential impact of the media and campaigns on their prospects (Huddy and Terkildsen 1993). Malcolm knew this, but she also knew that a female candidate cannot succeed with money and mobilization.

THE THIRD CORNERSTONE: MONEY

In *A Woman's Place Is in the House*, Burrell (1994) argued that party and organizational support, a well-trained campaign staff, and financial contributions were critical factors in women's campaigns. Scholars have found that early money (i.e., money given to candidates before the primary) can be especially important for female candidates (Francia 2001). In open seat and challenger races, these funds signal to other individuals and organizations that the candidate is viable. In the case of incumbents, a considerable war chest can be a significant deterrent to a primary challenge (Epstein and Zemsky 1995).

THE FINAL CORNERSTONE: MOBILIZATION

To be successful, female candidates require the support of women at other levels, most notably women voters. As mentioned in chapter 2, beginning in 1980, women voted in equal rates to men. Women's participation at the voting booth was critical to ELIST's mission, as women tend to be more liberal than men, are more likely to affiliate with the Democratic Party, and often seek descriptive representation—that is, electing someone "like them" to public office. But in 1992, relatively little was known about women voters in terms of data that could then be used to inform women's campaigns and affect the electoral system.[5]

ELIST's APPROACH TO THE FOUR CORNERSTONES

It is not simply a coincidence that the four areas that women and politics scholars highlighted as areas of concern are the very same areas that EMILY's List focused on in its post-1992 expansion. Over the next ten years, Malcolm reorganized and expanded the organization, creating several new programs and projects that transformed the organization into a multipronged interest organization with enormous influence in Democratic politics.

MEDIA, CAMPAIGNS, AND CANDIDATE CREDIBILITY

In 1993 ELIST tried to mediate the media-related problems that its candidates faced by creating a program to train candidates and campaign professionals. As a trained and experienced press secretary, Malcolm knew the impact of the media on electoral politics. She also knew that for women to win, they needed a support network, and professional consultants comprise a critical component of that network. "One of the few—as in perhaps a half-dozen-prominent female media consultants in the country" Dawn Laguens recently gave EMILY's List credit for helping more women enter the consultant field: "...more women are working their way into the pipeline, cutting their teeth on the kind of lower-profile races that will eventually qualify them for the big leagues. Having groups like EMILY's List, which seek out and train promising women for campaign work, doesn't hurt either" (Kornacki 2006, 40–42). Between 1993 and 2008, the organization trained "nearly 1,000 women and men" through their campaign training program, providing trainees with skills in campaign management, fundraising, media, research, and fieldwork.[6] In fact, EMILY's List provided a job placement program for trainees; in the 2000 election cycle, the organization placed 97 percent of its trainees into paying positions.[7]

In 2001 EMILY's List supplemented these efforts with a new program, Campaign Corps, which focused on training college students to work as support staff, "...in targeted progressive Democratic campaigns for the three months leading up to Election Day."[8] Campaign Corps dates back to the 1988 election cycle. Since that time, the program has "trained more than 500 young people in the basics of campaigning through both Campaign School and Mini-Camps."[9] Originally called Participation 2000, the program was funded by the Participation 2000 PAC, a PAC affiliated with the Democratic Party. In 2001 EMILY's List took over the administration and costs of the program.[10]

The decision to assimilate the Participation 2000 program into the larger ELIST organization and revamp it to serve the EMILY's List mission is a prime example of Malcolm's use of organizational learning to further the goals of the organization. She incorporated a preexisting program and adapted it to her ends, in this case providing viable female pro-choice Democratic candidates with trained campaign staff. Furthermore, the campaign-staff training and the Campaign Corps program further strengthened her ties with the Democratic Party organization. Trainings were conducted by political professionals whose names are familiar in Democratic circles: Mary Beth Cahill, campaign manager, John Kerry for President, and former executive director of EMILY's List; Steve Elmendorf, chief of staff, former House Minority Leader Richard Gephardt; Michael Meehan, director of message development and polling, Democratic National Committee; Marla Romash, Romash Communications, communications director for former Vice President Al Gore;

and Karen Tramontano, chief of staff, former President Bill Clinton.[11]

Since 1992, ELIST has put into place several programs to address the unique problems that female candidates face with the media and in campaigning. In large part, ELIST has addressed the credibility and campaign problems faced by female candidates by creating training programs for candidates, staff, and volunteers because a knowledgeable candidate and campaign team will be able to avoid or limit any negative impact of the media or the campaign process.

The next step in ELIST's expansion was to address the two remaining cornerstones blocking women's ascension to political power: money and mobilization.

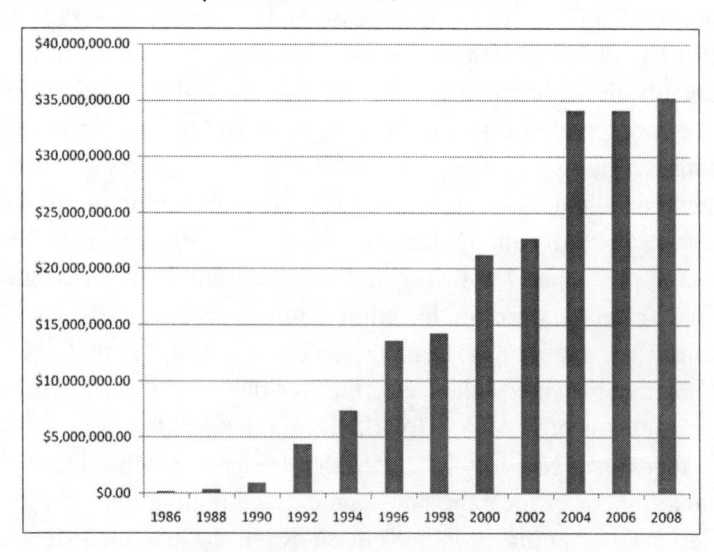

FIGURE 3.1. Receipts to EMILY's List, 1986–2008.

Source. Data from the Federal Election Commission.

Money and Candidate Credibility

From its inception through 2008, receipts to ELIST have continued to grow (see figure 3.1). Part of the explanation for ELIST's success is embedded in its endorsement process. By selecting candidates who have a high probability of winning, the organization has strengthened its position and power in electoral politics and its relationship with other organizations such as the Democratic Party. Given its strategic orientation, it is not surprising that only select female pro-choice Democratic candidates benefit from EMILY's List programs and contributions; only those who are considered *viable* become an ELIST-endorsed candidate. It is these lucky women who benefit from the full-service political organization that ELIST has become.

The Endorsement Process

Since the organization does not publicize all its endorsements but rather provides a list of endorsed candidates who have won, it is difficult to discuss specific endorsement decisions made by the organization in its early years.[12] Based on organizational literature, in 1986 the organization endorsed two candidates (EMILY's List 2009). Barbara Mikulski won her race and became the first woman elected to the U.S. Senate "in her own right"—that is, she was not elected to take the place of a deceased family member. But, thirty-three of the seventy women who ran for a seat in the U.S. Congress in 1986 were Democrats. Why did EMILY's List only endorse two?[13]

The organization's miniscule receipts and relative youth might explain its low number of endorsements in 1986. However, ten years later, in 1996, the organization boasted 45,000 members and just over $13 million in receipts but only endorsed forty-nine of the eighty-two female Democratic candidates for U.S. Congress.[14] ELIST is clearly selective in its endorsement of female pro-choice Democratic candidates. The purpose of this chapter is to provide the reader with a basic understanding of how the organization evolved from its origin as a donor network into a "full-service political organization." The specific factors that may affect candidate endorsement such as competition, partisanship of the district/state, and so on, will be addressed in chapter 5. At this point, it is important to understand the endorsement *process* and how that process changed as the organization expanded and transformed.

In the organization's early years, Malcolm and the Founding Mothers of ELIST raised money for female candidates by soliciting donations from within their social network(s). They relied on these friends to provide enough money to ensure that ELIST's endorsed candidates could mount a competitive campaign. As the organization's name implies, the focus was on providing endorsed candidates with "early" money to insure that others (the Democratic Party, PACs, and individuals) would provide additional support.

But twenty years later, the endorsement process seemed more vague and difficult. When one candidate asked ELIST for an endorsement, she was told that viability was critical and that the organization's assessment of viability relied heavily on how much money a candidate could raise during the first quarter of the cycle *without* EMILY's List support. More specifically, she was told that she needed to raise $250,000 to be considered viable.[15] In a 2007 interview, Ramona Oliver, communications director for EMILY's List, stated:

> We have what's called an assessment process. And we have a staff of people here who are responsible for doing nothing else but recruiting and assessing candidates. First of all, you have to be a woman, you have to be a

Democrat, you have to be pro-choice, which boils down to respecting the tenants of *Roe v. Wade*, which includes the core values of respecting a woman's privacy and the right to respect her life and health. We have a choice committee and a short questionnaire that the candidate fills out. The committee does an exhaustive assessment of a person's choice position. Lastly, you need to be running a viable campaign in a competitive race. Viability is based on a number of factors; it is really a measure of: if you can put together a strong campaign that can appeal to the voters and you're a good fit for the district. That doesn't necessarily mean that you had to run before. We look at the campaign operation. Are they putting together professional campaign operations with staff and a finance plan to raise the money with a voter contact and a field plan? Do they have a professional consultant team to help them? Our staff works with candidates to help them build a strong campaign operation. All of those factors go into viability assessment.[16]

In some ways, these criteria and this process seem at odds with the organization's mission and the barriers that female candidates face. In fact, that is one of the main reasons the organization formed. Why, then, is viability such an important part of the organization's endorsement criteria? The answer lies in the changes ELIST has made to its endorsement process and the changing definition and importance of viability in the organization's decision-making process.

CHANGES IN THE PROCESS

During ELIST's first active election cycle (1986), thirty-three Democratic women ran for federal office.[17] According to Congresswoman Rosa DeLauro (CT-4), the first executive director of EMILY's List, the candidate endorsement process in the early years of the organization centered on Malcolm.[18] As a keen political strategist, Malcolm and the other Founding Mothers often personally knew the candidates running for office; many also had experience as trained political consultants or Democratic Party operatives, which meant they had the political skills to evaluate a candidate's chances.[19]

But since 1992, the number of Democratic women running for federal office has increased exponentially. With upward of one hundred Democratic women vying for an EMILY's List endorsement each election cycle, Malcolm no longer relies on personal knowledge and "word on the street" to make endorsement decisions. As the organization grew and money became available to support multiple candidates from all over the country, the selection process became more sophisticated. According to organizational literature, an EMILY's List endorsement comes after a candidate:

> …has demonstrated that she is a viable, pro-choice Democratic woman…with a reasonable chance of winning base[ed] on our interactions with candidates and campaigns and on the expertise of and information gathered and analyzed by the EMILY's List political staff.…Candidates must be prepared to illustrate, credibly and specifically, how they can win—and demonstrate that they are taking those steps.…Candidates are also asked to fill out a short choice questionnaire to show their commitment to protecting the tenets of *Roe v. Wade*.[20]

Providing the candidate clears all these hurdles, she receives the endorsement of EMILY's List and all the corresponding benefits: mention in member newsletters and on the website, a political tracker, and a finance tracker.[21] She may receive direct and in-kind contributions ($5,000 per election, $10,000 per cycle), unlimited independent expenditures, direct mailings, and so on.

However, the only "promise" the organization publicly makes to the candidate is that, once recommended:

> ...a profile about the candidate and her race is sent to our members, who then decide whether to contribute to her campaign. There are generally a number of candidates included in a single candidate mailing. There is no regular schedule for mailings. Some candidates are included in more than one mailing. There is no standard amount of money that a candidate raises from a mailing as our members always choose which candidates to support.[22]

CHANGES IN CONTRIBUTIONS TO CANDIDATES

Not only has the ELIST endorsement process changed, but the type of funds ELIST provides to candidates has also changed. Data from *Vital Statistics on Congress* shows that a candidate running for a House seat between 1986 and 1994 needed (on average) between $359,577 and $686,198 to win. Senate races were even more expensive, with a win costing between $3,067,559 and $3,921,653 in the same period (Ornstein, Mann, and Malbin 2008). Time after time, candidates endorsed by ELIST have said that they would not have been elected without the help of ELIST.[23] Some of these accolades are for the organization's help with recruitment and training of both the candidate and her staff. But more often, candidates are referring to the direct or in-kind contributions from EMILY's List or the money it bundles from its membership.

An examination of the type of contributions ELIST gave to candidates over time provides more evidence of the transformation of the organization. Since its inception, ELIST has given its endorsed candidates a combined average of $3,208,919 per cycle in bundled money and PAC contributions. In terms of the

TABLE 3.1. EMILY's List PAC contributions to candidates (direct and in-kind) and bundled money, 1986–2008.

Year	PAC Contributions to Candidates	Bundled Money from Members
1986	$14,807	$0
1988	$70,647	$64,015
1990	$71,013	$198,575
1992	$348,007	$886,493
1994	$227,689	$822,015
1996	$253,218	$1,375,840
1998	$238,721	$1,734,556
2000	$221,746	$2,591,030
2002	$202,975	$6,198,169
2004	$120,535	$8,324,782
2006	$278,436	$8,239,439
2008	$244,951	$5,779,369

Source. Data from the Federal Election Commission and Congressional Quarterly's Political Moneyline.

types of monies given to candidates, as ELIST receipts have increased, it has provided more candidates in terms of direct contributions (cash) and in-direct contributions (services such as polling or a volunteer staff), as well as bundled money (see table 3.1). These funds and services from ELIST go a long way toward making a candidate competitive.

EARLY MONEY

EMILY's List was born, at least in part, out of Malcolm's frustration with traditional sources of funding for female candidates;

The Transformation of EMILY's List

one of Malcolm's main goals for EMILY's List was to give female pro-choice Democratic women money early enough to make them competitive.[24] Scholars have recognized the organization's role in giving candidates "early" money, defined as money received before the primary (Biersack et al., 1993; Burrell 1994; Conway 1991; Francia 2001).[25] The earliest money comes in during the first quarter, which is typically January through March of the election cycle (e.g., March 1999). The conventional wisdom is that EMILY's List supports female pro-choice candidates early.

Table 3.2 shows the number of candidates EMILY's List endorsed before and after the primary, as well as the win rate for those endorsed pre- and post-primary. In 2000 the organization stepped in after the primary to endorse a number of candidates, but in more recent years, the number of post-primary endorsements has declined. This is especially true for House races; it appears that EMILY's List makes decisions about Senate candidates earlier, picking up fewer candidates after the primary. This could be due to the higher cost of Senate races—EMILY's List needs to get involved earlier to make a difference. It is important to note that the early money that EMILY's List provides candidates is largely in the form of bundled checks that come in from EMILY's List members. According to data from the Federal Election Commission, 59 percent of endorsed candidates received bundled money before they received monetary support from the PAC.

An examination of the primary outcomes for female prochoice Democratic candidates during the period indicated there is a significant positive relationship between EMILY's List endorsement and primary victory ($r=.129$, $p=.01$).[26] EMILY's List candidates are much more likely to win their primaries than candidates not endorsed by the organization. Examining the win

TABLE 3.2. Number of candidates endorsed by EMILY's List by primary date and outcome, 2000–2008.

U.S. House of Representatives

Year	# Female Democrats in Primary	# Supported in Primary	% Supported in Primary	# Endorsed Who Won Primary	# Endorsed Post-Primary	# Endorsed Who Won General	% Endorsed Who Won General
2000	104	17	16.4%	15	22	22	59.4%
2002	113	24	21.2%	15	6	13	62%
2004	122	14	11.5%	12	2	8	57%
2006	141	28	19.9%	23	9	14	43.8%
2008	152	29	19.1%	24	8	15	40.5%

U.S. Senate

Year	# Female Democrats in Primary	# Supported in Primary	% Supported in Primary	# Endorsed Who Won Primary	# Endorsed Post-Primary	# Endorsed Who Won General	% Endorsed Who Won General
2000	11	5	45.5%	3	1	3	75%
2002	12	3	25%	3	2	5	0%
2004	15	7	46.6%	7	0	7	42.8%
2006	16	5	31.3%	5	0	5	100%
2008	7	2	28.6%	2	0	2	100%

Source. Data from the Federal Election Commission and the Center for American Women and Politics. The total number of endorsements in a year is equal to the number in column 2 of the House table, plus the number in column 6 of the House table, plus the number in column 2 of the Senate table, plus the number in column 6 of the Senate table.

rate for EMILY's List candidates in the general election, endorsed candidates won their races 55 percent of the time (on average) in the House and 54 percent (on average) in the Senate.

Given that viability is one of the factors the organization claims to be critically important to its endorsement decision, one would expect this rate to be higher. Clearly, other factors beyond just EMILY's List endorsement are at work in these races; these factors will be fully explored in chapter 5. For now, it is important to recognize that EMILY's List remains devoted to giving early money to its candidates while also recognizing that the endorsement process has become complicated.

WOMEN-VERSUS-WOMEN RACES

One example of such a complication is woman-versus-woman races. Although not officially stated, it is a popular belief that EMILY'S List has a policy of not getting involved in primaries where two or more female pro-choice Democratic women are running against each other.[27] Data on EMILY's List endorsement of candidates engaged in woman-to-woman races in a Democratic primary between 2000 and 2008 indicate that this is not always the case. EMILY's List endorsed a candidate in thirty-three of sixty-six primary races involving two female Democratic women during this period. More often than not, these races were primaries that involved challenger or open seat races. In terms of EMILY's List's impact, of the women who received a pre-primary endorsement, even though they were running against another female Democratic candidate, 63 percent of endorsed candidates won their primary. Of those, 67 percent won their general election race.[28]

EMILY's List's involvement in Democratic primaries involving two female Democratic candidates is not altogether new, but it is not the norm. According to Ramona Oliver, communications director for EMILY's List: "If we really assess that race and we don't think any of the women will emerge from the primary unless we get in and endorse, then we'll start the process of trying to decide who to endorse and then it's based on the kind of campaign and the viability of the campaign."[29] For example, in 1992, EMILY's List endorsed Geraldine Ferraro in the primary, even though her primary opponent, Elizabeth Holtzman, was also a female pro-choice Democrat. According to Clift and Brazaitis (2003), EMILY's List made this decision because, "Holtzman was a spoiler with no real chance of winning the nomination or of beating D'Amato" (54). A congresswoman who sought an ELIST endorsement in a primary against another woman was turned down until she raised $250,000. "At that point—the point that I raised that much money and had won the primary—I didn't need EMILY's List's help."[30] The organization *did* end up endorsing her and bundling money to her, but she did not see that money as critical to her election given that her real hurdle occurred in the primary.

It is logical that a strategic organization seeking to maximize its success and influence would shy away from primaries with two or more female Democratic candidates given the organization's mission: as long as the winner is a pro-choice Democratic woman, EMILY's List does not care *which* woman wins. In other primary situations, however, where there is only one female Democratic woman running, we expect to see a higher amount of EMILY's List activity, especially since the organization is known for giving "early" money. As the pool of female Democratic candidates continues to grow and EMILY's List support becomes more coveted, the organization will face this pressure more often.

Candidate Mailings

Group membership—and therefore receipts and influence—waxes and wanes according to changes in the political environment, such as majority control of Congress, legal decisions regarding organization activity, or changes within organizations such as a change in leadership or the relevance of the interest to members and/or the public (Green and Bigelow 2005; Patterson and Singer 2002). EMILY's List has escaped this cycle because of Malcolm's strategic leadership, which has allowed the organization to point out its real success. As the perception of it as a successful organization increases, its membership also expands.

How do individuals come to view EMILY's List as a successful organization? First, and perhaps the most critical element to EMILY's List's success, is the existence of candidates as patrons such as Barbara Mikulski, Nita Lowey, and Gwen Moore. Walker (1991) argued that patrons provide organizations considerable legitimacy. As these successful female candidates (and other women) give Malcolm and the organization credit for their electoral victories, they link the organization's success to the success of its endorsed candidates.

Second, the organization's press coverage is overwhelmingly positive, and this positive press is bolstered by the organization's aggressive strategy of contacting members.[31] The ELIST staff views the organization's mailings as one of the most valuable aspects of an ELIST endorsement. It is through these mailings that the organization provides members with information about its candidates.

An exploration of the organization's mailings during the 2008 election cycle provides some insight into the content and frequency of the organization's outreach efforts. During that cycle, the organization sent twenty-six mailings to members.[32] Nineteen included information about the organization's efforts through its WOMEN VOTE! program and the organization's efforts in the Political Opportunity Program (POP). All attacked the record of President Bush or another Republican politician, including Vice President Cheney, talk-radio host Rush Limbaugh, 2008 vice-presidential candidate Sarah Palin, and Senator John Sununu (the opponent of one of ELIST's candidates).[33] More than half had a candidate recommendation or solicitation for support as the lead story; only two focused on organizational news.

In the past decade, the organization has expanded its outreach to members by supplementing these traditional mailings with email and web-based newsletters. In the first three months of 2007 alone, EMILY's List sent fourteen emails: five mentioned Bush, Cheney, or the Republican Party in the subject line; one referred to Speaker Nancy Pelosi; and one entitled "First Woman President," touted its endorsement of Senator Hillary Clinton for President in 2008. All included requests for money and most emphasized the impact of the organization or its endorsed candidates. For example, on January 31 an email entitled, "More the Same from Bush" stated:

> The failed Bush agenda is hurting Americans. The only remedy is to bring new progressive leadership to Washington. That's why, every single day, EMILY's List is working hard to elect even more pro-choice Democratic women to office—women who will protect our rights and defend our values for years to come, no matter who is in the White House.[34]

It went on to list the goals of EMILY's List in the upcoming election cycle, including recruiting new candidates, "defending our pro-choice women leaders from outrageous Republican attacks," supporting incumbents, training activists, and planning the "largest get-out-the-vote operation ever in what will be the most important presidential election of our lifetime."[35]

Regardless of the format, these mailings play a critical role in the organization's strategy. They keep donors connected to the organization, inform them of the organization's connection to and perspective on current events, and most importantly, serve to reinforce and mobilize EMILY's List members.

MOBILIZATION

Members are an important part of EMILY's List's success. In order to provide endorsed candidates with funds, the organization must draw in members. Yet women—EMILY's List's target audience—are small-time players in the world of moneyed politics. The gender gap in political donations is long-standing and well-documented (Burns et al. 2001; Francia et al. 2003; Green et al. 1999). But ELIST's total receipts indicate that the organization has found a way to overcome this obstacle.[36] The key is mobilization, which stands as the fourth cornerstone of ELIST's expansion and transformation.

Mobilization is critical to ELIST's success. Due to its structure as a PAC, the organization and its endorsed candidates rely on donations from individuals who believe in the mission and goals of the organization. But ELIST's success is also dependent on the mobilization of voters and on the mobilization of women willing to run. The mobilization of voters and candidates will be the focus of the remainder of this chapter. The next chapter focuses on evaluating EMILY's List's mobilization of members.

WOMEN VOTERS

Malcolm knew that female candidates needed female voters—after all, many blamed the Republican takeover of the House in

1994 on the decline in Democratic women voting in that election. Malcolm knew that ELIST needed to mobilize women voters, but she also knew it had to be approached strategically. The organization needed women who supported the substantive and descriptive goals of the organization or who could be targeted to make these preferences more salient.[37] As Snow et al. (1986) found, with enough knowledge about a target audience, any issue or set of issues can be framed in an appealing manner. But effective targeting and ultimately the success of the organization and its candidates required reliable scientific research on female voters, and few organizations had the money to do this type of research.[38]

To rectify this gap in knowledge, in 1996, ELIST commissioned the first *Women's Monitor* to:

> ...build a comprehensive data file on the political views and voting behaviors of American women. In addition to survey research and focus groups, the *Women's Monitor* helped pioneer other innovative techniques including micro-targeting, voter modeling and techniques to dispel myths about women voters and candidates.[39]

The organization claims that "EMILY's List candidates and Democrats at large have come to depend upon the reliable, objective information in the *Monitor*."[40]

Since 1996, EMILY's List has used data from the *Women's Monitor* to inform its WOMEN VOTE! project (discussed in chapter 2). Also known as AMERICA WOMEN VOTE!, portions of this program are sometimes funded through a joint fundraising committee, a financial partnership between EMILY's List and one of the national Democratic Party's congressional committees (DCCC and DSCC) or various state-level Democratic Party organizations, depending on the election year.[41] For example, in

2004, ELIST had three joint fundraising committees: AMERICA WOMEN VOTE! with the DCCC[42]; AMERICAN WOMEN VOTE! 2002 with various state Democratic Party committees[43]; and South Dakota WOMEN VOTE!, a joint fundraising committee between EMILY's List and the South Dakota Democratic Party, where Stephanie Herseth was engaged in a hotly contested House race.[44] Table 3.3 provides a breakdown of projects completed by the WOMEN VOTE! program since its inception.

It is impossible to track the specifics of how these funds were used because the committee's disbursements appear only as transfers from the joint fundraising committee to the various affiliated committees. Once the money enters the organization's coffers, it becomes incorporated in the amorphous pool of soft money the organization can use for GOTV efforts. One way to assess the amount of resources the organization devotes to

TABLE 3.3. EMILY's List WOMEN VOTE! projects, 1994–2008.

Year	Individuals Contacted	Pieces of Mail	Phone Calls	# of Target States
1994	902,575	–	–	1
1996	2.7 million	+7.5 million	500,000	31
1998	3.4 million	+80 million	+2 million	26
2000	–	10,281,120	+2 million	7
2002	–	6,630,906	1,989,562	18
2004	954,890	3,411,520	1,423,641	4
2006	–	468,336	79,603	21
2008	6.5 million	+2.5 million	+1 million	16

Source. Data for 1994 is from a "prototype" program in CA. Data acquired from EMILY's List.

state-level activities is by examining its non-federal expenditures (see table 3.4), which are funded, at least in part, through soft money contributions from individuals. Since these activities occur at the state level and pertain to state-level elections, they do not have to be itemized in FEC records, but the FEC *does* require the organization report the gross amount spent on non-federal activities.[45]

FEC records indicate that EMILY's List's state-level work took off in 1994, and like the organization's overall receipts and membership numbers, its state-level activities have consistently increased as well. It is interesting to note that of the other women's PACs discussed in chapter 2, only the Women's Campaign Forum uses its PAC to fund non-federal activities.[46]

TABLE 3.4. EMILY's List non-federal expenditures, 1986–2008.

Year	Non-Federal Expenditures
1986	$-
1988	$-
1990	$-
1992	$284,201
1994	$-
1996	$1,166,466
1998	$3,572,349
2000	$6,719,801
2002	$5,561,400
2004	$8,123,514
2006	$7,782,580
2008	$9,904,135

Source. Data from the Federal Election Commission.

EMILY's List Mobilizes Future Candidates

While EMILY's List's federal activity has garnered it the most attention, both the original women's PACs and ELIST have recognized the importance of having a "farm team" of women in the states. As with other parts of the ELIST model, Malcolm began the state-level project in a slow piecemeal manner.

In 1990 the organization endorsed Ann Richards who was running for governor of Texas. The creation of the WOMEN VOTE! program (as discussed previously) became a critical component of ELIST's state-level work because it put the organization's staff and volunteers into contact with innumerable local women, informing them about the organization, its goals, its candidates, and the necessity of their involvement.[47] The implementation of a GOTV program requires a significant amount of information about state and local politics, including voter data, issue preferences and salience, and so on. Successful GOTV programs also require knowledge of and relationship with local political actors, whose connections with groups and members of the community are critical.

When the number of female Democratic women in state legislatures dropped in 2000, the knowledge and experience that EMILY's List acquired in the WOMEN VOTE! programs during the 1996, 1998, and 2000 election cycles became the foundation for the organization's launch of a full-scale state-level program called the Political Opportunity Program (POP) in 2001.[48] Through the POP program, EMILY's List broadened its support network and built up the number of women running for office across the country. POP was the final piece of ELIST's puzzle in some ways; as one organization staffer put it at EMILY's List's anniversary luncheon in 2005, ELIST has a mom with Ellen Malcolm and now it has a "POP."[49]

POP's mission is straightforward: "to recruit, train, and support pro-choice Democratic women running for state legislative, constitutional and key local offices."[50] To fulfill this mission, using its experiences with the WOMEN VOTE! program, ELIST split the country into regions and assigned a regional director and a team to each. Just three years later, the organization claimed that over 3,100 women had been trained through the POP program.[51] POP was even more successful in the 2008 cycle, training more than 1,300 people and helping "175 pro-choice Democratic women candidates in 32 states win, including 10 statewide candidates. POP candidate and California Assemblywoman Karen Bass became the first African American woman speaker of a state legislature in U.S. history."[52]

Table 3.5. EMILY's List political opportunity activities, 2002–2008.

Election Cycle	Candidates Elected	Individuals Trained
2002	86	961
2004	140	–
2006	194	–
2008	175	1,300

Source. Data acquired from EMILY's List.

The POP program is based on Malcolm's belief in building campaigns from the ground up. Media coverage of POP training portrays the training as very hands-on:

> At a recent training session in Miami, Coyne-McCoy [a regional director of POP] guided about 30 women in a hotel conference room through the fundamentals of

raising money: how to form an organized plan and target groups of donors such as friends, voters who share your beliefs, people who hate your opponent and community powerbrokers. Participants received a thick training manual that covers every aspect of running a professional campaign, down to minute details such as a 15-page spread sheet with Florida press contacts, sample door-knocking guides and estimated costs for direct mail pieces—to the cent. (Thomas 2004)

In offering these services, EMILY's List provides potential candidates with critical information that helps them become viable candidates and increases the chances that the Democratic Party organizations and PACs will support them in the future. Unfortunately, there is no way to fully assess just how much the organization spends on these trainings, how many women are trained, how many actually run for office or how many win, except to rely on the organization's accounts.[53] Unfortunately, further exploration of EMILY's List activity on the state level requires data collection beyond the scope of this project. What appears to be a decline in the sheer number of candidates endorsed by the organization at the federal level could reflect a strategic redeployment of resources toward state-level work. Exploring the organization's state-level activity would be a worthwhile and interesting endeavor for future scholars.

ELIST AND SWIFTBOATING

During the 2004 presidential election, a 527 organization called Swift Boat Veterans and POWs for Truth spent $22.5 million on negative advertisements regarding presidential candidate John Kerry's service in Vietnam.[54] "Swiftboating" and "527s" became household words, although this type of organization had existed for several years. Referred to as "stealth PACs" by some,

527s are political organizations that collect donations and make expenditures to "influence or attempt to influence the selection, nomination, election or appointment of an individual to a federal, state, or local public office or office in a political organization."[55]

Four years prior, Malcolm formed a 527 organization, EMILY's List Non-Federal.[56] The existence of an affiliated 527 provides EMILY's List with two benefits: First, individuals can give unlimited amounts of money to 527 committees; considering that ELIST began as a donor network funded entirely by money from wealthy, well-connected, and politically savvy women, this provides wealthy ELIST members with another way to use their money to help achieve the organization's substantive and descriptive goals. Second, 527 funds can be used in ways that PAC funds cannot. It may be easiest to think about 527 organizations as the PAC version of a "soft money" system. In fact, 527s are widely thought of as a way to avoid the BCRA prohibition on soft-money donations to national party committees (Boatwright 2007).

EMILY'S List is not the only PAC to have created a 527, but its ability to do so is of fundamental importance to the organization. The importance that EMILY'S List places on its 527 is evidenced by a recent court case brought by EMILY's List against the FEC in reaction to the Commission's recent ruling that limited the types of funds 527s can use.[57] According to IRS reports, in 2002, EMILY's List Non-Federal reported receipts of just over $4 million; by 2008, receipts to the 527 reached over $13 million (see table 3.6).[58] In 2004 the Center for Responsive Politics (CRP) listed EMILY's List's 527 as number 13 in the Top 50 527s; in 2006 and 2008, EMILY's List Non-Federal was in the Top 5.[59] It is interesting to note, however, that CRP does not have ELIST listed as a "Major Player 527" in any of these years.

At this point, EMILY's List has not used the 527 to pay for electioneering, which would require it to file separate reports

TABLE 3.6. Receipts to EMILY's List 527, 2002–2008.

Year	Receipts
2002	$4,006,195
2004	$7,739,546
2006	$11,776,201
2008	$13,659,955

Source. Data from the Internal Revenue Service.

to the FEC; thus, its activity is as opaque as that paid for by "non-federal expenditures."[60] The IRS reports, however, provide a general sense of the broad categories of spending. In 2002 just under 25 percent of the 527's spending went to overhead costs.[61] Thus, EMILY's List's 527 appears to function like a "parent" organization of a connected PAC, without the limitations of that legal relationship. If this is the case, by creating the 527, Malcolm was able to overcome just one more obstacle to ELIST's success: its non-connected status. As mentioned in chapter 2, when ELIST formed, its non-connected status set it apart from the other women's PACs and could have hampered the organization's growth. To avoid that, Malcolm marketed ELIST as a donor network until after 1992, when it had grown enough in terms of members and receipts to be sustainable. EMILY's List's creation of the 527 provided a way to lessen the burden of its overhead costs, and thus further strengthen the organization.

The 527 is also important to ELIST's growth insofar as it covers some of the costs associated with the organization's GOTV efforts. In 2008 the largest amount of expenditures made by the 527 ($9.8 million of the $13+ million) were transfers to the ELIST PAC for the federal portion of the organization's GOTV efforts.[62]

According to Weissman and Hassan (2006), until recently the FEC "refused to subject 527s to contribution restrictions so long as their campaign ads and voter mobilization programs steered clear of formal candidate endorsements" (79). Having the 527 pick up some of the mobilization costs associated with various ELIST programs helps utilize the hard money donations received by the organization in the most effective way. For example, EMILY's List's formation of its 527 could very well be a key element in the organization's decision not to conduct the same amount of issue advocacy in 2002 (via the PAC) that it engaged in during 2000. ELIST did not step away from pull back on its issue advocacy in 2002; rather, instead of paying for issue advocacy with hard dollar contributions to its PAC, EMILY's List Non-Federal paid for it.[63]

Malcolm's decision to form the 527 may be the best example yet of her propensity to experiment with new ideas and strategies, especially if they have been shown by others to be effective. It is important to note that rarely does Malcolm simply copy what others are doing; rather, she adapts strategies to fit her own ends and to compensate for problems that others encounter. In this way, Malcolm's decision-making process is a product of double-loop learning (Argyris 1996; Dodd 1994).

EMILY's List and the Internet

Malcolm's most recent experiment—TEAM EMILY—asks members to do more than simply write a check and attend a luncheon or retreat. Through this online community, the organization attempts to create a dialogue with members through online chats, opinion polls, and event listings, as well as provide a more general resource for members to obtain information about the activities of endorsed candidates and even discuss things with other members. The website also offers ELIST a convenient way to make last-minute pleas for money if endorsed candidates are embroiled in a particularly competitive election (Sanchez 2004; Taylor 2004; Walsh 2004). Malcolm hopes that TEAM EMILY will help recruit "…a new generation of activists [through] building an online grassroots community."[64]

TEAM EMILY is another example of Malcolm's willingness to utilize a strategy others had profited from (i.e., Internet technology) and mold it to her needs. But it also exemplifies Malcolm's desire to adapt the organization's strategy to keep in step with societal changes. While most of ELIST's large donors may not be drawn to social networking sites and may not be comfortable sharing information on the Internet, younger members and potential members must feel that the organization is not only relevant to their interests but is also on the cutting edge. In 2007 EMILY's List created a presence on the popular social networking Web site Facebook; by mid-2009 it had over 7,000 fans.[65] In June 2008, the organization hired a new Internet director, Emily Lockwood, to focus on:

> …expanding the organization's online presence by engaging new supporters, raising money, and promoting EMILY's List candidates. The internet director also manages all elements of the organization's online program including www.emilyslist.org, email communications, blogger outreach, and promotion on external website. (EMILY's List 2008)

Prior to EMILY's List, Lockwood was the Internet director for online giving in Hillary Clinton's 2008 presidential campaign (EMILY's List 2008).

EMILY's List and the Democratic Party: Part Two

Chapter 2 included a brief discussion of the relationship between EMILY's List and the Democratic Party vis-à-vis the exchange of funds. When asked about the organization's relationship with the Democratic Party, Communications Director Ramona Oliver cited several other ways in which ELIST and the Democratic Party work together. She reported that the organization is now drawing members who are more devoted to Democratic ideals than feminist ones: "We are a pretty critical piece of the puzzle for Democrats in general, so major Democratic voters, men and women who recognize that fact, have also begun to support us. It's a function of our success."[66] Oliver also discussed the relationship with the congressional campaign committees, which she admitted can sometimes be strained:

> ...very often we are in the primaries. We are the only one on the woman's side. Very often, the party establishment will still line up with one of the guys we are running against. But there's not any acrimony in that process; it's just that's the way it is.[67]

Oliver indicated that the biggest shift in the relationship between ELIST, the Democratic Party, and Democratic-leaning organizations began in 2004:

> With the passage of BCRA, you had the wall go up between Democratic organizations, the Democratic Party, and the campaigns. So you had all of these external groups like EMILY'S List, the AFL, and the Sierra Club out here doing their separate thing. The Republicans typically run a much more centralized effort and had a great deal of control. It was really that level of diversity that we have with our audiences that we finally, as Democrats,

really harnessed. So AMERICA VOTES!, actually more so than America Coming Together (ACT), really created a vehicle for all of the different Democratic institutions and organizations to come together, coordinate their work, remove redundancy, and make it more streamlined. Through AMERICA VOTES! began this wonderful collaboration of research and information. Our WOMEN VOTE! director went to all the meetings and helped with working with all of these other organizations on the independent side. We've also caught up to the Republicans on the technology side in terms of microtargeting. EMILY's List literally helped pioneer that for Democrats. So there is a much greater level of cooperation and coordination and effectiveness out there on the ground with these groups, which probably did not exist before. We have a lot more coordination on the national level, as well as among the state teams now too.[68]

Conclusion

As an organization, EMILY's List presents something of a moving target. Although its mission has remained steadfast and its senior leadership has remained amazingly stable, the organization has acted and reacted in a dynamic way to changing social and political circumstances. Its dynamism is evidenced in the relationship that Malcolm built between ELIST and the Democratic Party. While that relationship can be complicated at times—most notably when ELIST supports one primary candidate and the Party establishment supports another—Malcolm and the other Founding Mothers firmly believed ELIST should align itself with the Democratic Party, as they viewed the Democrats as most receptive to the full integration of women in the political system, not to mention the organization's stance on abortion. It is this belief that led ELIST to become a party adjunct, and the ties between the organization and the Democratic Party continue to play a critical role in the organization's ability to influence American politics.

The dynamic nature of the organization is also evident in its relationship to its members. What began in the mid-1980s as pseudo Tupperware parties built on a preexisting social network of politically interested women, expanded into member luncheons and conferences in the 1990s, and provided the foundation for the creation of online communities and grassroots activism in the new millennium. ELIST's success in this regard is connected to its use of identity politics to convince women that they are a critical part of the political system and mobilize them to become more involved and better represented. It is this growth in EMILY's List's membership that is the focus of the next chapter.

Endnotes

1. EMILY's List. 2009. Where we come from. http://emilyslist.org/about/where_we_come_from/(accessed October 17, 2009). Nita Lowey, who received $40,000 from EMILY's List in 1992, stated, "They've been extremely helpful for me....They get people to contribute, and all you have to do is say thank you" (*The Houston Chronicle* 1992). Also see Schwawrtz and Cooper 1992.
2. Summary of women candidates for selected offices 1970–2008: Major party nominees. 2008. Center for American Women and Politics: Fact sheet. http://www.cawp.rutgers.edu/fast_facts/elections/documents/can_histsum.pdf (accessed January 5, 2009).
3. The amount of candidate contributions given by ELIST to candidates in 1992 is from data acquired from the Federal Election Commission at www.fec.gov.
4. Summary of women candidates for selected offices 1970–2008: Major party nominees. 2008. Center for American Women and Politics: Fact sheet. http://www.cawp.rutgers.edu/fast_facts/elections/documents/can_histsum.pdf (accessed January 5, 2009).
5. See Conway (1985) for one exception.
6. Campaign staff training and jobs. 2007. EMILY's List. http://emilyslist.org/programs/campaign_jobs/ (accessed January 5, 2009).
7. Campaign staff training and jobs. 2007. EMILY's List. http://emilyslist.org/programs/campaign_jobs/ (accessed January 5, 2009).
8. About Campaign Corps. 2007. EMILY's List. http://emilyslist.org/programs/campaign_corps/about/ (accessed January 5, 2009).
9. About Campaign Corps. 2007. EMILY's List. http://emilyslist.org/programs/campaign_corps/about/ (accessed January 5, 2009).
10. Campaign Corps. 2008. EMILY's List. http://www.emilyslist.org/programs/campaign_corps/2008_campaign_corps/ (accessed January 5, 2009); Faculty biography: Sean Gagen. 2009. The George Washington University: The graduate school of political management. http://www.gwu.edu/~gspm/about/bios/gagen.html (accessed January 5, 2009); Contributions received by: Participation 2000, INC. 1999. Federal Election Commission.

http://query.nictusa.com/cgi-bin/com_rcvd/1999_C00221887 (accessed January 5, 2009); Contributions of EMILY's List. 2001. Federal Election Commission. http://query.nictusa.com/cgi-bin/com_rcvd/ 2001_C00221887 (accessed March 1, 2005).

11. Campaign staff training and jobs. 2007. EMILY's List. http://emilyslist.org/programs/campaign_jobs/ (accessed January 5, 2009).
12. More recent endorsements are accessible by tracking the organization's financial contributions via FEC data, a process discussed in detail in chapter 6 and in the appendix.
13. Summary of women candidates for selected offices 1970–2008: Major party nominees. 2008. Center for American Women and Politics: Fact sheet. http://www.cawp.rutgers.edu/fast_facts/elections/documents/can_histsum.pdf (accessed January 5, 2009).
14. Membership figures from EMILY's List 2009. Data on the organization's receipts comes from records of the FEC at www.fec.gov. Data on the candidates endorsed by EMILY's List in 1996 comes from CQ Political Moneyline at www.fecinfo.org.
15. Interview with member of House of Representatives, October 30, 2005. Requested anonymity. This definition of viability was echoed by prominent Democratic fundraiser Terry McAuliffe during an interview on National Public Radio (NPR). The host asked McAuliffe the secret of viability to which he replied, "…cash on hand." National Public Radio: Morning edition. 2007. McAuliffe: Shorter 2008 race speeds fundraising. http://www.npr.org/templates/story/story.php?storyId=7292720&sc=emaf (accessed January 5, 2009).
16. Personal communication with Ramona Oliver, Communications Director for EMILY's List, April 2008.
17. http://www.cawp.rutgers.edu/fast_facts/elections/documents/can_histsum.pdf.
18. Personal communication with Congresswoman Rosa DeLauro (D-CT), October 2005.
19. Personal communication with Ramona Oliver, April 2008; personal communication with Joanne Howes, April 2008; personal communication with Judith Lichtman, June 2008.
20. Personal communication with former EMILY's List staff member, October 2006.

21. Organizational literature references political and finance trackers. Political trackers are there to help every female Democratic pro-choice candidate. If a candidate makes it into the "endorsed" category, then the organization also assigns a finance tracker to the campaign to handle fundraising: including writing a fundraising plan, hiring staff, training the candidate and staff regarding effective fundraising strategies, and so on.
22. Personal communication with former EMILY's List staff member, October 2006.
23. "20th Anniversary Gala Luncheon: Barbara Mikulski. 2005. Emily's List. http://www.youtube.com/watch?v=9P5KobkPy94&feature=related (accessed May 1, 2009). 20th Anniversary Gala Luncheon: Rosa DeLauro. 2005. Emily's List. http://www.youtube.com/watch?v=aq8VheelG_0&feature=channel (accessed May 1, 2009). 20th Anniversary Gala Luncheon: Gwen Moore. 2005. Emily's List. http://www.youtube.com/watch?v=f40kQMo8451&feature=channel_page (accessed May 1, 2009). More can be found at http://www.youtube.com/profile?user=emilyslist&view=videos&start=40.
24. Both Joanne Howes and Judith Lichtman, two of the Founding Mothers of EMILY's List, mentioned these as part of the rationale for creating EMILY's List. Personal communication with Judith Lichtman, June 2008. Personal communication with Joanne Howes, April 2008.
25. A large caveat here is that "early" money could be coming from the organization in the form of bundled contributions from members to the candidate, not money from the organization itself.
26. These figures represent the correlation coeffcent and the p-value where $p=0.01$ is highly significant.
27. Author interview with female Democratic member of Congress, October 2005. Requested anonymity.
28. Primary results were obtained from the Center for American Women and Politics (www.cawp.rutgers.edu). CAWP does not provide primary vote totals but just states whether a candidate won or lost the primary. Consequently, I cannot statistically evaluate the competitiveness of the primary elections in the same manner. A competitive race is one in which the candidate received between 45 percent and 55 percent of the vote in the election.

29. Author interview with Ramona Oliver, communications director of EMILY's List, April 2007.
30. Interview with female member of Congress, October 31, 2005. Requested anonymity.
31. An examination of articles in the *New York Times, Washington Post, Los Angeles Times, The Hill,* and *Roll Call* from 1986–2004 show a consistent pattern of positive coverage.
32. See appendix for coding guide.
33. Personal communication.
34. Personal communication.
35. Personal communication.
36. Francia et al. (2003) based their findings on a randomized sample of congressional donors taken from the population of donors in 1996. It is possible that donors to ELIST are significantly different from donors to congressional candidates, albeit some ELIST donors would be included in the population of congressional donors used by Francia et al. because of their bundled contributions. Nevertheless, as discussed in the next chapter, more than 80 percent of donors to ELIST are women, and these donors provided the organization with more than $35 million in the 2008 election cycle.
37. The use of targeted appeals in campaigning was not new, but deploying these appeals through direct mail campaigns was a recent development (Sabato 1981).
38. Although there was ongoing academic research on female voters (Conway 1985), it took longer to become public and usually was not useful in microtargeting voters.
39. n.d.(e). Women's monitor. EMILY's List. http://www.emilyslist.org/newsroom/monitor/ (accessed May 9, 2007).
40. n.d.(d). Women's monitor: Fact sheet. EMILY's List. http://www.emilyslist.org/newsroom/monitor/monitor_fact_sheet.html (accessed May 9, 2007).
41. See records of the FEC at www.fec.gov.
42. Reports image index for committee ID: C00397919 (American Women Vote!). 2005. Federal Election Commission. http://images.nictusa.com/cgi-bin/fecimg/?C00397919 (accessed May 1, 2009).

43. Reports image index for committee ID: C00377994 (American Women Vote!). 2002. Federal Election Commission. http://images.nictusa.com/cgi-bin/fecimg/?C00377994 (accessed May 1, 2009).
44. Reports image index for committee ID: C00397000 (South Dakota Women Vote!). 2005. Federal Election Commission. http://images.nictusa.com/cgi-bin/fecimg/?C00397000 (accessed May 1, 2009); and EMILY's List. 2004. Insider News. http://www.emilyslist.org/happening/insider-news/20040603.html (accessed December 1, 2005).
45. Non-connected committees that have established separate federal and non-federal accounts under 11 CFR 102.5 (a)(1)(i), or that make federal and non-federal disbursements from a single account under 11 CFR 102.5(a)(1)(ii), shall allocate their federal and non-federal expenses in the following way: their administrative expenses, costs of generic voter drives, and costs of public communications that refer to any political party, with at least 50 percent federal funds, as defined in 11 CFR 300.2(g). (1) If federal and non-federal funds are collected by one committee through a joint activity, that committee shall allocate its direct costs of fundraising, as described in paragraph (a)(2) of this section, according to the funds received method. Under this method, the committee shall allocate its fundraising costs based on the ratio of funds received into its federal account to its total receipts from each fundraising program or event. This ratio shall be estimated prior to each such program or event based upon the committee's reasonable prediction of its federal and non-federal revenue from that program or event, and shall be noted in the committee's report for the period in which the first disbursement for such program or event occurred, submitted pursuant to 11 CFR 104.5. Electronic code of federal regulations: Title 11-federal elections. http://a257.g.akamaitech.net/7/257/2422/01jan20061500/edocket.access.gpo.gov/cfr_2006/janqtr/11cfr106.6.htm (accessed March 5, 2007).
46. This is not to say that these other organizations do not participate at the state and local level. However, both the NWPC and NOW/PAC are part of organizations with state and local chapters that can fund these activities separate from the federal PAC (Barakso 2005; Woods 2001).

47. This is from organization press releases referring to helping eight women attain the office of governor. See: Women We Helped Elect. *EMILY's List.* EMILY's List: Women we helped elect. EMILY's List. http://www.emilyslist.org/candidates/women-helped.html (accessed on May 30, 2009).
48. EMILY's List: Latest POP victories. 2009. EMILY's List. http://www.emilyslist.org/do/pop/index.html (accessed May 30, 2009).
49. Personal experience at EMILY's List 20th anniversary luncheon.
50. EMILY's List: Women we helped elect. EMILY's List. http://www.emilyslist.org/candidates/women-helped.html (accessed on May 30, 2009).
51. EMILY's List: Latest POP victories. 2009. EMILY's List http://www.emilyslist.org/do/pop/index.html (accessed May 30, 2009).
52. EMILY's List: Where we come from. 2009. EMILY's List. http://emilyslist.org/about/where_we_come_from/ (accessed June 1, 2009).
53. As mentioned in the discussion of ELIST's WOMEN VOTE! program, even though these activities are funded with money from the federal PAC, they are categorized as non-federal expenditures that do not have to be itemized. An alternative route to this information is through state-level campaign finance records in states where trainings are held, a project beyond the scope of this book.
54. Swift boats and POWs for truth: Overview. 2008. Open Secrets: Center for Responsive Politics. http://www.opensecrets.org/527s/527cmtedetail.php?cycle=2008&ein=201041228. Accessed June 1, 2009.
55. Exemption requirements: Political organizations. 2008. Internal Revenue Service. http://www.irs.gov/charities/political/article/0,id=96350,00.html (accessed June 1, 2009). According to the FEC, Unincorporated, unregistered '527' organizations may also make electioneering communications, subject to the disclosure requirements and the prohibition against corporate and labor funds. See Electioneering communications: '527' organizations. 2009. Federal Election Commission. http://www.fec.gov/pages/brochures/electioneering.shtml#527s (accessed June 1, 2009). Further, the FEC states that "Persons who make electioneering communications that aggregate more than $10,000 in the calendar year must file the "24 Hour Notice of Disbursements/Obligations for Elec-

tioneering Communications" (FEC Form 9) with the Commission within 24 hours of the disclosure date. 11 CFR 104.20(b). FEC Form 9 must be *received* by the Commission by 11:59 p.m. on the day following the disclosure date."
56. Internal Revenue Service Form 8771. Department of the Treasury: InternalRevenueService.http://forms.irs.gov/politicalOrgsSearch/search/Print.action?formId=4771&formType=6E71 (accessed May 18, 2009).
57. EMILY's List v. FEC. 1981. Federal Election Commission. http://www.fec.gov/law/litigation_CCA_E.shtml (accessed May 18, 2009).
58. EMILY's List IRS Form 990. 2002. Department of the Treasury: InternalRevenueService.http://forms.irs.gov/politicalOrgsSearch/search/generatePDF.action?formId='521391360-990POL-01'&formType=P90 (accessed May 18, 2009).
59. 527s committees: Top 50 federally focused organizations. 2008. Open Secrets: Center for Responsive Politics. http://www.opensecrets.org/527s/527cmtes.php?level=C&cycle=2008 (accessed May 18, 2009).
60. Electioneering communications reports. 2009. Federal Election Commission. http://www.fec.gov/finance/disclosure/ec_table.shtml (accessed May 18, 2009). Organizations or individuals doing electioneering have to report to the FEC (fn 131). EMILY's List did not appear in an examination of these records. 527 refers to the section of the Internal Revenue Service Code that governs the organization's behavior. Exemption requirements: Political organizations. 2008. Internal Revenue Service. http://www.irs.gov/charities/political/article/0,,id=96350,00.html (accessed June 1, 2009).
61. EMILY's List IRS Form 990. 2002. Department of the Treasury: InternalRevenueService.http://forms.irs.gov/politicalOrgsSearch/search/generatePDF.action?formId='521391360-990POL-01'&formType=P90 (accessed May 18, 2009).
62. 527s Committees: EMILY's List Non-Federal: Expenditures, 2008 Cycle. 2008. Open Secrets: Center for Responsive Politics. http://www.opensecrets.org/527s/527cmtedetail_expends.php?cycle=2008&ein=521391360[(accessed May 18, 2009).

63. Correspondence between Cynthia D. Morton (FEC) and Michael B. Blumenfeld (IRS). 2006. Federal Election Commission. http://www.fec.gov/pdf/nprm/lobbying/comm10.pdf (accessed May 18, 2009).
64. EMILY's List: Frequently asked questions. 2007. EMILY's List. http://www.emilyslist.org/team_emily/FAQ.html (accessed March 01, 2007); EMILY's List. Where we come from. http://emilyslist.org/about/where_we_come_from/ (accessed October 17, 2009).
65. More information on EMILY's List Facebook page can be found at: http://www.facebook.com/emilyslist.
66. Personal communication with Ramona Oliver, communications director for EMILY's List, April 2008.
67. Personal communication with Ramona Oliver, communications director for EMILY's List, April 2008.
68. Personal communication with Ramona Oliver, communications director for EMILY's List, April 2008.

CHAPTER 4

MEMBERS AND THEIR ORGANIZATIONAL ROLES

Using data from the FEC, this chapter focuses on donors to EMILY's List over an eight-year period (from 2000–2008). After providing a brief descriptive analysis based on the information available in FEC records, I examine what EMILY's List has done to reverse the gender gap in political contributions, transforming women into powerful political donors in the same way that Ellen Malcolm transformed the organization from a donor network into a multipronged influence organization.

INTRODUCTION

Malbin (2003) suggested that money and politics are caught up in a push-pull relationship. Money is either pushed into the system by persons or groups seeking access and influence, or it is pulled into the system by candidates, parties, and PACs who want the legitimacy that money can buy. For single-issue or ideological groups to be effective, this push-pull relationship must occur synergistically: while pulling in money from contributors, they must simultaneously find ways to push their money into the political arena. More specifically, they have to make sure their money *matters*.

To a large degree, the ability to *matter* is dependent on how much money they have to disburse. If a group can give money to politicians and parties, it makes them take notice. Similarly, if the group can point to several thousand members who are organized and will mobilize for or against an individual or policy, a pragmatic candidate or legislator will pay attention.

EMILY's List possesses both of these things: money *and* members. In the years immediately following the formation of EMILY's List, the Founding Mothers nurtured the fledgling organization, pouring their money into it and talking about it to their friends. Slowly the membership grew, and by the time the organization celebrated its first victory—the election of Barbara Mikulski (D-MD) to the U.S. Senate—the membership of ELIST had grown to 1,155 (EMILY's List 2009). This slow strategic start made the organization strong and stable so that when opportunity knocked in 1991, ELIST was ready to welcome new members. In that year, membership grew more than 600 percent, and this growth facilitated the organization's transformation from a donor network to a multipronged influence group with strong ties to the Democratic Party (EMILY's List 2009).

While EMILY's List is now cast as a "heavy hitter," little attention has been paid to the organization's members who provide the organization with its astounding receipts (CRP 2009).

There are several explanations for the lack of scholarly attention to ELIST membership. First, although the organization boasted of more than 100,000 members in 2008 (EMILY's List 2009), the number of dues-paying members is much smaller.[1] If, in fact, ELIST is an organization with Beltway appeal that does not translate to the far reaches of the country, then scholarly inattention to the organization and its membership makes sense. Studies of elite political donors and their motivations already exist (Green et al. 1999; Francia et al. 2003). In their study of donors to EMILY's List and other women's PACs in 1996, Day and Hadley (2005) found ELIST membership to be largely female (94 percent).[2]

Scholars of campaign finance have shown that female donors are a rarity, not the norm. Yet rather than see EMILY's List as a way to gain insight into the motivations of female donors, it seems that scholars have decided that ELISTers and the EMILY's List organization are not unique enough to merit interest. But, in fact, the opposite is true. The study of EMILY's List and its membership provides insight into the mobilization of female political donors. Since EMILY's List's mission and appeals are driven by identity politics, stressing the need for women to use their political power at all levels of government and society, those drawn in by these appeals are participating in decades-old debates about gender inequalities and the steps women should take to stop further inequalities (Lorber 2005).[3] Furthermore, the transformation of the organization in the late 1990s could have affected the composition of the organization's membership.[4] It is not unrealistic to expect more men to see ELIST as a way to push their money into the political arena or to use the organization to achieve their partisan goals.

After briefly reviewing the research on political donors and interest-group membership, this chapter focuses on the demographic characteristics of ELIST's members, followed by a discussion of ELIST's membership over time.

POLITICAL DONORS

Political donors—that is, individuals who give money in order to affect an election—are typically considered an elite group of individuals motivated by the opportunity to gain political access and influence. That perspective changed, however, when scholars discovered the impact of political donations on political participation and its implication for political equality (Burns, Schlozman, and Verba 2001). Those who donate to political campaigns were more likely to vote and volunteer, were more likely to persuade others, and generally exhibited higher levels of political efficacy.[5] They also comprise a very small percentage of the total population.

According to the Center for Responsive Politics, only .61 percent of the U.S. adult population gave $200 or more in the 2008 election; less than one-third of those donors were women.[6] This is not surprising, as the gender gap in contributing to political campaigns is long-standing and well-documented (Burns et al. 2001; Francia et al. 2003; Green et al. 1999). Reminiscent of the explanations given for the gender gap in representation, the gender gap in political contributions has multiple causes. First, women are most disadvantaged in political activity when such activity involves resources such as money; if women were as "well endowed" as men, there would be less of a gender gap in campaign finance (Schlozman et al. 1999). Scholars have found that that if age, income, number of dependants, "age" of money, pension status, and health were held constant, the donor gap would disappear (Capek 1998).

In the real world, such factors cannot be held constant—the gap does exist and it *matters!* Green et al. (1999) argued that female donors bring "a distinctive voice" to campaign finance; female donors tend to be more Democratic, more likely to hold liberal positions, and more motivated by policy concerns than male donors. Furthermore, they found that female and male donors give to a "different mix of candidates," with women actually giving to a greater number of candidates but in smaller amounts. The female donor pool is also rather static. Francia et al. (2003) found little to no change in the percentage of women participating in 1978 when compared to the donor pool in 1996; in both years, women comprised roughly 17 percent of congressional donors.

Those most likely to donate to congressional candidates are white, wealthy men with high levels of education (Francia et al. 2003, 33). Members of this elite group can be further categorized according to the frequency of contributions and motivation. *Occasional donors* come into and out of the donor pool; they are often motivated to give by personal appeals and they are more likely to participate in local or state politics than federal politics. They tend to limit their contributions to a few candidates and/or races, and often give smaller aggregate amounts. Occasional donors often fall into the "ideologue" category—that is, ideological rather than material concerns motivate them to give (53). *Habitual donors* behave in the opposite way—they donate in practically every election and usually give significant amounts (22). Francia and colleagues found some evidence that a significant portion of habitual donors were "loyal" to a certain candidate or candidates for long periods of time. Female donors tend to fall into the occasional donor category.

The Benefits of Group Membership

PAC donors may have different motives than congressional donors. Donors to congressional or even presidential candidates give because they want to affect the outcome of the election(s) and/or they want to purchase access to the candidate. While some PAC donors can share these motives, when individuals give to ELIST they are also joining an *organization* and thus should be understood by applying current theories of political donations and the motives that drive group membership.

The literature examining why individuals join groups dates back to the mid-1960s when Mancur Olson (1965) persuasively argued that obtaining and retaining members required a group to provide those members with incentives. Olson focused on economic incentives, in part because at the time the largest and most prolific groups were those associated with businesses or labor, both of which sought material gains. Since that time, Olson's theory has been expanded upon; membership incentives now include purposive and solidary benefits (Wilson 1973; Walker 1991; Moe 1980) as well as material benefits.

It is these last two types of benefits that factor into ELIST's membership and mobilization. According to Wilson (1973), purposive benefits are those that come from joining a group because of its position on issues or because it helps elect candidates with whom one shares a particular ideological or political perspective. The main type of benefits ELIST provides its members are purposive. By joining the organization and supporting its endorsed candidates, an ELIST member can simultaneously have his or her policy preferences represented and help elect more Democrats into office.

The second type of benefit that ELIST provides its membership with is solidary benefits. Solidary benefits refer to the creation of professional or social networks that come from joining a group. Like any rational group, the more money a member gives, the more solidary benefits he or she can obtain. For example, for $200 and a promise to give a bundled check of $200 or more to at least two endorsed candidates each cycle, an individual can become a member of ELIST. As a member, he or she receives the organization newsletter, candidate endorsement mailings, and invitations to the organization's yearly luncheon. This is a solidary benefit. These meetings give members the opportunity to meet and network with like-minded men and women, as well as interact with endorsed candidates.[7] For a membership fee of $1,000 per year and the promise to bundle $200 or more to two endorsed candidates, an individual can obtain even more solidary benefits, including a spot on the Majority Council. Members of the Majority Council receive all the benefits associated with regular membership as well as an invitation to a weekend-long retreat where members have the opportunity to interact with each other, interact with candidates and the organization's leadership, and hear from top campaign professionals.

Are ELISTers Donors or Members?

As mentioned earlier, individuals who give money to PACs, especially non-connected PACs such as EMILY's List, have not been considered "different enough" by scholars to merit extensive examination. But just as EMILY's List is unique, so too are its adherents. In some ways, they are simply donors; in other ways, they are clearly members. For example, the organization acts like a membership-based interest group in the sense that it retains donors by providing purposive and solidary benefits to its members. EMILY's List also functions like a membership organization in that it does extensive outreach in the form of mailings and advertising to retain members.

However, unlike a traditional membership organization where individual members can directly influence the organization's decisions and trajectory, the only power EMILY's List members possess is the ability to withhold donations.[8] This is a considerable amount of influence. Due to EMILY's List's formal status as a PAC, not a 501(c)(3) nonprofit that can accept grant or foundation money, ELIST must mobilize its members in order to survive. With that much power, it is important to fully understand who belongs to EMILY's List.[9]

Data and Method

The bulk of these data comes from FEC records. Political organizations and candidates are required to provide the FEC with basic demographic information for all donors who give $200 or more each year.[10] Donations from individuals who give less than $200 an election are reported in lump sums as "un-itemized contributions." Bundled or earmarked contributions are reported on the organization's reports; these contributions have to be itemized, although there are different standards of disclosure depending on the amount of the contribution.[11] Those bundled contributions of $200 or more are itemized and reported on the FEC filings and designated as "earmarked" contributions.[12] The FEC does not require organizations to provide itemized information about bundled contributions of less than $200. The following discussion, therefore, is limited to individual contributions to the organization and/or bundled contributions to endorsed candidates of $200 or more.

Using FEC records, I compiled a dataset of every donation to the organization (not bundled) from 2000 to 2008. Using a series of Access queries, I created a list comprised of the discrete individuals who gave to the EMILY's List PAC during this period (see appendix for detailed methodology). Creating this list was a cumbersome process; in some years, one individual might give upward of fifteen separate donations over the course of the election cycle. These data were further coded for gender, occupation, state of residence, level of contribution, and donor status (whether the donor was "new" to EMILY's List or a repeat donor). Repeat donors were further categorized as "loyalists" who contributed $200 or more in every cycle after joining the organization or occasional donors who gave at least one more contribution during the period but did not give in *each* subsequent election. The results of this process will be used in the following for a comparison of EMILY's List members to our current knowledge about the basic characteristics of political donors.[13]

Basic Demographics

Sex

Given the purpose and ideological perspective of the organization, it is unsurprising that women comprise more than 80 percent of the organization's membership over the past eight years (see table 4.1). However, this is also the first indication that the transformation of EMILY's List may have affected the composition of its membership, as Day and Hadley (2005) found that women comprised upward of 94 percent of ELIST donors in 1996.[14]

Using these data to explore the composition of ELIST membership over time, it is apparent that the membership of EMILY's List vis-à-vis the sex of the donors appears to have changed. Whereas in 2000, 97 percent of EMILY's List donors were women, by 2008 women comprise a smaller percentage

TABLE 4.1. EMILY's List donors by sex, 2000–2008.

Year	% of Female Donors	$ from Women	% of Male Donors	$ from Men
2000	97%	$6,323,647	3%	$172,645
2002	89%	$9,550,365	10%	$1,050,323
2004	86%	$10,895,147	12%	$1,448,013
2006	86%	$13,964,652	12%	$1,952,529
2008	87%	$10,109,235	11%	$1,239,464

Note. Data compiled from records of the Federal Election Commission. These figures will not match the figures for all donors or all receipts, as these data represent only large donors (those who give $200 or more) and those whose first names match the list of male and female last names used for coding. Any donor with missing data was excluded from the analysis for this chart. Thus, the rows do not always equal 100 percent.

of EMILY's List members, although they still dominate. The male membership of EMILY's List rose from approximately 3 percent in 2000 to 11 percent in 2008. Starting in 2002, male EMILY's List members provided the organization with over $1 million in donations.

What accounts for the increase in male membership? First, male participation in feminist groups and liberal women's movements dates back to the women's suffrage movement in the mid-1800s. Men participated in the 1848 Seneca Falls Convention and were active participants in the woman suffrage movement, although men were excluded from voting and leadership positions (McGlen et al. 2004). There were also male members of women's organizations created during the second-wave women's movement, such as the National Organization of Women, that welcomed members of both sexes.

However, it is doubtful that the increase in male membership of EMILY's List is the result of a rise in the number of feminist men. Rather, as EMILY's List transformed from donor network to multipronged influence organization with deep connections to the Democratic Party, more people, especially men, came to view the organization as a legitimate source of influence. Joining EMILY's List became another way of supporting one's partisan agenda. Founding mother, Joanne Howes, observed this trend as well:

> EMILY's List attracts donors who are interested in getting women to office, but it also attracts donors who are just interested in Democratic victories. They know that EMILY'S List is committed to Democratic victory. They see EMILY'S List as a vehicle because they [EMILY's List] do such a good job training, getting candidates the right campaign staff, etc. Some of the donors to EMILY'S List are not opposed to women having power, but it is not necessarily their core belief.[15]

Occupation

In some analyses of political donors, occupation is used an explanatory variable. For example, Burns et al. (2001) found that occupation had a significant impact on whether or not an individual participated in various types of political behavior because of the skills associated with certain jobs, not to mention the money and social networks. Francia et al. (2003) found that business executives (48 percent) supplied congressional candidates with the majority of their individual donations, followed by attorneys (17 percent), and those in the medical (13 percent) and education (11 percent) professions (Francia et al. 2003, 28). Only 6 percent of respondents in Francia's sample chose "retired," "other," or "none" as their occupation, even though 40 percent of donors surveyed were over the age of sixty.[16]

The largest occupational categories for EMILY's List donors during this period are "retired," "none," and "self-employed" (see table 4.2).[17] The existence of retired persons in the donor pool fits with what we know about the relationship between age and political behavior. The majority of "retired" persons fall into an age cohort that: 1) already participates in politics at a higher rate and thus will be more numerous, and 2) often has more disposable income than those in younger cohorts. The fact that 19 percent of EMILY's List donors identify themselves as retired is understandable. In fact, this percentage should increase over time as the long-time members of the organization—veterans of the women's movement of the 1960s and 1970s—reach retirement age.

TABLE 4.2. Occupational status of EMILY's List donors, 2000–2008.

Occupation	Percent of Membership	Average Donation to PAC (Not Bundled)
Self	13%	$1,566.85
Home	4%	$1,414.41
Retired	19%	$1,382.36
Business	10%	$1,332.29
Other	10%	$1,155.09
Government	1%	$1,151.83
Legal	4%	$1,064.61
Education	8%	$1,042.59
Medical	3%	$785.64
None	26%	$685.20

Source. Data from the Federal Election Commission.
Note. Incomplete data excluded from analysis; therefore, column 3 does not equal 100 percent.

The single largest occupational category (an average of 26 percent of all donors) is "none," which includes those individuals who left the occupation line blank as well as those who listed "none" or "n/a."[18] Clearly these donors have to possess some source of income; otherwise, they would be unable to give over $200 to an organization. It is possible that these donors are, in fact, independently wealthy individuals who are not employed in traditional ways. For example, in the FEC online database, Malcolm's occupation is listed as "none" on some records and as "EMILY's List" on others. On the other hand, donors who fall into this category gave EMILY's List the smallest average contribution of all donor occupation categories, an average contribution of $685.20 during the 2000–2008 period.

Independently wealthy individuals such as Malcolm are much more likely to list "self" as their occupation, which is the third largest category of EMILY's List donors during the 2000–2008 period. Not only do self-employed individuals comprise 13 percent of ELIST's membership during this period, they also provide the highest average contribution: $1,566.85 (see table 4.3). Individuals who work in the business world (financial or business sectors) comprise a significant percentage of ELIST's large donor pool (10 percent) and provide a relatively high average contribution, which fits with their higher rate of pay and higher rate of wealth in general.[19]

The second highest average contribution from ELIST members (an average contribution of $1,414) came from those who listed "home" (or some version of home) as their occupation.[20] The amount of their contribution is disproportionate to their composition in the membership, as only 4 percent of donors to EMILY's List between 2000 and 2008 fell into this category. However, the level of support these women and men gave to the organization speaks to EMILY's List's success in mobilizing and politicizing women and men across the country. I would also expect that these individuals would comprise a greater percentage of the organization's total membership if these data also included information on smaller donors.

What these data make clear is the diversity of EMILY's List membership in terms of occupation. Although EMILY's List donors are predominately female, they come from a range of occupations, including business, medical, legal, and education. This bodes well for the organization's longevity, as these occupations are shown to help individuals acquire wealth and skills at a greater rate than other occupations. If the organization continues to mobilize these members, they could provide significantly more money to the organization and its candidates in future cycles.

Residence
Further evidence that EMILY's List appeals to a wide range of individuals can be seen by examining the residential patterns of EMILY's List donors.[21] These data provide important insights into the diversity of EMILY's List membership during the past eight years.[22] The idea that EMILY's List has limited geographic appeal is incorrect; from 2000–2008, EMILY's List drew members from all over the country (see table 4.3) (Friedman 1993).[23]

While the organization does have a national membership, over 60 percent of EMILY's List large donors during the 2000–2008 period came from ten states, five of which are the most populous states in the United States (California, Texas, New York, Florida, and Illinois). These five states alone provided EMILY's List with an average of 43 percent of its large donors during the eight-year period. There is little indication that the

TABLE 4.3. EMILY's List members by state, 2000–2008.

State	2000	2002	2004	2006	2008	Average
CA	21.50%	21.40%	19.90%	20.60%	20.80%	20.84%
NY	13.20%	12.00%	11.00%	11.20%	11.00%	11.68%
MA	5.80%	5.70%	7.90%	6.00%	5.80%	6.24%
FL	4.30%	4.90%	5.40%	5.40%	5.00%	5.00%
TX	5.20%	5.20%	4.70%	4.50%	4.90%	4.90%
IL	4.20%	4.10%	4.10%	4.10%	4.00%	4.10%
MD	3.90%	4.50%	4.20%	3.60%	4.30%	4.10%
DC	4.60%	4.80%	3.70%	3.20%	3.60%	3.98%
WA	4.10%	2.90%	3.30%	3.50%	3.20%	3.40%
PA	3.20%	3.20%	3.50%	3.50%	3.30%	3.34%
VA	3.10%	3.70%	3.30%	3.10%	3.20%	3.28%
NJ	2.70%	3.00%	2.80%	2.90%	2.70%	2.82%
MI	2.00%	2.70%	2.50%	2.90%	2.30%	2.48%
CT	2.20%	2.10%	2.20%	2.40%	2.30%	2.24%
CO	1.80%	1.60%	1.90%	2.00%	2.50%	1.96%
OH	2.20%	1.70%	1.80%	1.80%	1.80%	1.86%
AZ	1.00%	1.30%	1.60%	1.60%	1.60%	1.42%
NC	1.20%	1.10%	1.50%	1.30%	1.80%	1.38%
OR	1.00%	1.10%	1.30%	1.70%	1.50%	1.32%
GA	1.50%	1.30%	1.20%	1.40%	1.20%	1.32%
MN	1.20%	1.20%	1.30%	1.30%	1.40%	1.28%
WI	1.40%	1.20%	1.00%	1.10%	0.80%	1.10%
MO	0.70%	0.90%	1.20%	1.10%	1.20%	1.02%
NM	0.90%	1.00%	0.80%	1.20%	1.00%	0.98%
NH	0.50%	0.50%	0.60%	0.60%	0.70%	0.58%
IN	0.60%	0.50%	0.50%	0.60%	0.70%	0.58%
ME	0.30%	0.50%	0.60%	0.70%	0.60%	0.54%
TN	0.40%	0.50%	0.50%	0.70%	0.50%	0.52%

(continued on next page)

TABLE 4.3. (continued)

State	2000	2002	2004	2006	2008	Average
KY	0.40%	0.50%	0.50%	0.50%	0.40%	0.46%
VT	0.50%	0.50%	0.40%	0.40%	0.50%	0.46%
SC	0.30%	0.30%	0.40%	0.40%	0.60%	0.40%
IA	0.30%	0.30%	0.40%	0.40%	0.40%	0.36%
KS	0.20%	0.30%	0.50%	0.40%	0.40%	0.36%
RI	0.30%	0.30%	0.30%	0.40%	0.40%	0.34%
NV	0.30%	0.30%	0.30%	0.30%	0.40%	0.32%
AR	0.50%	0.20%	0.30%	0.20%	0.30%	0.30%
HI	0.10%	0.20%	0.30%	0.30%	0.40%	0.26%
LA	0.40%	0.20%	0.20%	0.20%	0.30%	0.26%
OK	0.20%	0.20%	0.30%	0.30%	0.30%	0.26%
UT	0.10%	0.40%	0.30%	0.30%	0.20%	0.26%
DE	0.30%	0.30%	0.30%	0.20%	0.20%	0.26%
WV	0.20%	0.20%	0.20%	0.20%	0.20%	0.20%
NE	0.20%	0.20%	0.20%	0.20%	0.20%	0.20%
AL	0.20%	0.20%	0.20%	0.20%	0.20%	0.20%
ID	0.10%	0.20%	0.20%	0.20%	0.20%	0.18%
AK	0.20%	0.10%	0.20%	0.20%	0.20%	0.18%
MT	0.10%	0.10%	0.20%	0.20%	0.20%	0.16%
WY	0.10%	0.10%	0.10%	0.10%	0.20%	0.12%
SD	0.00%	0.10%	0.10%	0.10%	0.10%	0.08%
MS	0.10%	0.10%	0.00%	0.10%	0.10%	0.08%
ND	0.00%	0.00%	0.00%	0.10%	0.00%	0.02%
VI	0.00%	0.00%	0.00%	0.00%	0.10%	0.02%

Source. Data from the Federal Election Commission.

placement of ELIST's membership is related to the political culture of members vis-à-vis women's participation in politics. Only one of these top-ten ELIST donor states makes the list of top-ten states for female members of the state legislature. There also exists a wide range in terms of how many women the state has currently serving in Congress—California's congressional delegation of fifty-three includes twenty-two women, whereas Massachusetts's congressional delegation of eight includes one woman.[24]

Another possible explanation for geographical distribution of ELIST's membership is that individuals who live in states where the organization has endorsed a federal candidate during the period were more exposed to the organization and its mission through ELIST's GOTV efforts and thus will be overrepresented in the donor pool.[25] In terms of the relationship between candidate support and membership, the data are clear: 95 percent of donations came from states where EMILY's List supported a candidate during the 2000–2008 period (see table 4.4). Unsurprisingly, the relationship between the percentage of ELIST members from that state and ELIST's endorsement of a candidate from that state is positive, strong, and significant ($r=.77$; $p=.000$). Still, the relationship is not perfect. Although California and New York provide ELIST with almost 32 percent of its membership and have a high number of ELIST candidates, the organization has also made a number of key endorsements in FL and OH but those states have few members within their borders.

Malbin and Gais (1998) found that political donations increase as the competitiveness of the election increases; perhaps ELIST donors are more plentiful in areas with a greater number of ELIST candidates engaged in competitive elections. However, these data suggest that this is not the case. During the 2000–2008

TABLE 4.4. EMILY's List members and endorsed candidates by state, 2000–2008.

State	Rank of State in ELIST Donors	Rank of State for Sending Women to Congress	# of Women in Congress	Rank of State Legislature	# of ELIST Endorsed Candidates	# of ELIST Endorsed Candidates in Competitive Seats
CA	1	1	22	16	24	4
DC	8	50	1	n/a	1	0
FL	4	4	6	25	14	4
IL	6	5	6	17	9	5
MA	3	15	1	18	1	0
MD	7	19	2	9	3	0
NY	2	3	7	23	12	4
PA	9	6	2	46	6	4
TX	5	2	4	25	1	0
WA	10	13	3	6	4	3

Source. Data from the Federal Election Commission, the Center for American Women and Politics, and Congressional Quarterly.

period, EMILY's List endorsed 184 candidates in the primary or general election cycle. According to data from Congressional Quarterly, only 72 of these candidates (39 percent) were engaged in a competitive election. Furthermore, even though all of the top-ten states (in terms of ELIST membership) had at least one EMILY's List candidate running for office during the period, only candidates from six of those states were engaged in competitive races (see table 4.5).

Examining the geographic representation of ELIST members provides two insights. First, these data leave little doubt that EMILY's List has a national donor base and is well-placed to pull donors, especially women, into the political system, as discussed in greater detail in the following section. Second, these data suggest that categorizing individuals who belong to EMILY's List as donors is ill-advised. While all of the data and analysis up to this point cast Malcolm and the leadership of EMILY's List as the organization's driving force, the strong relationship between donors' state of residence and the organization's decisions vis-à-vis candidate endorsements should not be dismissed too quickly.

Although the relationship between EMILY's List endorsements and members' state of residence may simply be the result of successful targeting, it may also be indicative of the motives of EMILY's List members. Political donations and group membership can be the result of an individual seeking substantive, descriptive, and/or geographic representation, as discussed in chapter 2. Until now, an EMILY's List membership was not commonly considered an effective means for seeking geographic representation. However, these data suggest that EMILY's List's growth could be tied to its ability to offer its members a way to obtain all three types of representation simultaneously, not to mention the additional purposive and solidary incentives associated with membership.

The discovery that EMILY's List provides these types of benefits to its membership provides further evidence that EMILY's List is not a typical PAC or "checkbook" organization that individuals donate to and forget about. Rather, it is a multipronged influence organization that offers unique incentives to members, gives unique services to candidates, and has a unique relationship with the Democratic Party.

Types of ELISTers

According to Francia et al. (2003), very few political donors are "perpetual" or "habitual" donors, giving to the same candidate repeatedly. Data on EMILY's List membership during the 2000–2008 cycle indicates that a significant portion of ELIST members *are* habitual donors, or loyalists. Of the 8,697 ELIST members in 2000, 1,217 (13.8 percent) became loyalists, giving $200 or more to the organization during each of the subsequent election cycles examined. Performing this same tracking procedure for donors in 2002–2008, the existence of a growing loyal membership is clear.

New Donors

During the past four election cycles, EMILY's List added over 16,000 new donors into the organization's large donor pool (see table 4.5). The organization added more new donors during the two midterm election cycles (2002 and 2006) than during the two presidential election cycles examined (2004 and 2008).[26]

The conventional wisdom in campaign finance scholarship is that new political donors are rare; most of the money given by individuals is from those who have given in previous cycles. In *Election after Reform*, Malbin (2006) found an unexpectedly

TABLE 4.5. Percentage of new and repeat donors to ELIST by election cycle, 2002–2008.

Year	% of New Donors	% of Repeat Donors
2002	62.6%	37.4%
2004	42.0%	58.0%
2006	47.3%	52.7%
2008	31.6%	68.4%

Source. Data from the Federal Election Commission.

large number of new donors (78.8 percent) in the 2004 donor pool; in fact, he noted that the parties were having great success recruiting new donors as early as 2003. Corrado (2006) argued that the influx of new donors in 2004 was likely the result of the passage of the Bipartisan Campaign Reform Act (BCRA) in 2002, which banned the parties from raising soft money. In reaction to BCRA, the political parties expanded their efforts to bring in hard money contributions from individuals. While this might explain the expansion of the donor pool in 2004 in terms of political parties, data from EMILY's List suggests that the organization's ability to pull in new donors predates the 2004 cycle, nor is there any indication that ELIST's newbie phenomenon is tied to BCRA. Rather, ELIST's ability to draw in new members is more reflective of the organization's unique structure and activities.

Sex, Location, and Money

As expected, women comprise a larger percentage of the Newbies and repeat ELIST members than men. That said, the percentage of men who become repeat donors to ELIST has slightly increased during the period, from 16.7 percent to 21.7 percent. As mentioned before, the goals and ideological position of the organization is becoming more appealing to men; certainly "feminist men" are ripe for donating to EMILY's List (Conover 1988; Cook and Wilcox 1991; Kaufmann and Petrocik 1999). Men may perceive EMILY's List as an increasingly legitimate outlet for their money due to Malcolm's connection with other Democratic-leaning organizations such as America Coming Together (ACT) and the Democratic National Committee, or the degree to which the organization has engaged in more "mainstream" political activities as discussed in chapters 2 and 3.[27]

Newbies generally live in the same states as Repeat members, which is not surprising since ELIST has a national membership with large donors in practically all the states. It seems likely that information about EMILY's List is being passed through formal and informal networks, as it has from the beginning. There is little evidence from interviews or organizational materials that EMILY's List has engaged in major recruitment activities or membership drives during this time period, though it is likely that the organization's GOTV activities act as *de facto* membership drives. Given the apparent relationship between donor residency and ELIST candidate endorsements, it makes sense that new donors would come from the same areas as current donors.

Newbies gave significantly less money to ELIST than repeat donors (see table 4.6). Clearly, EMILY's List relies on repeat donors to provide "major" donations. It is possible that the first time an individual donates, it is in a smaller amount, but subsequent donations are higher amounts as the donor develops trust and a "stake" in the organization's success.[28] This is borne out by looking at Newbies who become Repeat or Loyalist donors in subsequent cycles.

TABLE 4.6. Amount of money given to EMILY's List and candidates (bundled) by election cycle, donor sex, and donor type, 2002–2008.

Year	Total Donors	Total Given	% Female	% Male
2002				
New	5,325	$17,362,453	70.8%	11.9%
Repeat	3,186	$38,878,166	83.2%	8.3%
Total	8,511	$56,240,619	75.5%	10.6%
2004				
New	3,304	$18,194,706	76.6%	23.4%
Repeat	4,562	$87,872,406	80.9%	19.1%
Total	7,866	$106,067,112	79.1%	20.9%
2006				
New	5,541	$41,529,921	67.3%	32.7%
Repeat	6,183	$91,542,367	78.6%	21.4%
Total	11,724	$133,072,288	73.2%	26.8%
2008				
New	2,553	$3,425,682	80.0%	20.0%
Repeat	5,532	$20,831,692	78.3%	21.7%
Total	8,085	$24,257,374	78.8%	21.2%

Note. Data from the Federal Election Commission. These figures will not match the figures for all donors or all receipts as these data represent only large donors (those who give $200 or more) and those whose first names match the list of male and female last names used for coding. Included in these data are individuals who just gave bundled contributions, which accounts for the disparity between these data and the data in table 4.1.

Conversions

In examining the conversion of donors during the 2000 to 2008 election cycles, two cycles years stand out. Of the 5,369 Newbie donors in 2002, 1,832 (34.1 percent) became occasional donors, whereas 845 (15.7 percent) became Loyalists. However, in 2004, the conversion rate changed dramatically. Of the 3,325 new ELISTers in 2004, 1,717 (51.6 percent) became Loyalists and the remainder became occasional donors, donating again in either the 2006 or the 2008 cycle. The fact that 100 percent of the new ELISTers of 2004 remained active with the organization in subsequent cycles is unexpected. This is likely the result of the extensive outreach and effort by multiple political actors in that cycle to recruit and retain donors. In 2006 ELIST's conversion rates stabilized; of the 5,541 new donors in 2006, 1,788 (32.3 percent) became occasional donors. What percentage of these individuals will become Loyalists by giving to the organization in 2010 remains to be seen.

The second change occurred in 2008. In that cycle, Newbies only comprised 31.6 percent of EMILY's List's donor pool, down from 47 percent in the previous cycle (see table 4.7). There are several possible explanations for why the 2008 cycle brought fewer new donors into the EMILY's List fold. Malbin (2004) claimed that new donors "are [more drawn to] personalities or issues than institutions" (184). Whereas in 2006, the organization's greater focus on partisan politics brought donors into the organization's ranks, in 2008 the organization's endorsement of Hillary Rodham Clinton and its participation in the hotly contested Democratic presidential primary created somewhat of a backlash (see chapter 6) (Pappu 2008).[29] Determining the cause of the ebb and flow in new large donors to EMILY's List is beyond the scope of this book, but this does provide a starting point for future scholars interested in the

TABLE 4.7. Conversion of Newbies by election cycle, 2002–2006.

Year	To Loyalists	To Occasional
2002	33.7%	15.7%
2004	51.6%	48.4%
2006	32.2%	–

Source. Data from the Federal Election Commission.

behavior and decision making of political donors and interest-group members.

CONCLUSION

One goal of this chapter was to provide yet another way to understand EMILY's List. Scholars examining the role of organizations tend to focus on leadership and structure. While these are obviously critical elements—without Malcolm's leadership and vision, it is doubtful that the organization could have evolved into the multifaceted influence organization it is today—it is the members who provide a critical link between the organization and the outside world. These women and men are power brokers, albeit non-traditional ones, *and without their contributions,* the organization would not have the money to pursue its goals.[30]

Without members, some might view EMILY's List as a plaything of a rich female politico. Yet given the broad base of the organization in terms of sex, location, occupation, and donations, there is no doubt that EMILY's List is a growing, dynamic organization. The fact that it has managed to recruit and retain a significant number of new large donors to the organization in each of the past five cycles speaks to the strength of its leadership and strategy. The fact that the vast majority of these new ELISTers are women makes this feat even more remarkable, as women are not known as political donors. ELIST's phenomenal ability to pull in new donors may be that because the organization is not just a PAC but also an interest group, a party adjunct, and a campaign organization. Furthermore, the organization provides not just incentives but the opportunity for many donors to acquire substantive and descriptive, if not geographic, representation which is seen as key to circumventing the obstacles female donors face.

The members of EMILY's List provide yet another example of the organization's impact on composition and content of American political life. It is this view of the organization—as a reckoning force—that guides the next chapter. There I explore the impact of the organization on congressional elections. It is in this arena that the organization's adaptation and evolution is clear. An empirical investigation of the strategies used by and an examination of how those strategies are affected by the political environment will solidify EMILY's List's position as an adept political organization, comfortable with using whatever tools necessary to achieve its goals and meet the needs of its members.

Endnotes

1. For example, data from the FEC and Congressional Quarterly's Political Moneyline indicate that 13,814 individuals contributed $200 or more to the organization during the 2004 election cycle (which is the minimum membership dues requested by the organization).
2. In their examination of the policy interests and ideological agenda of donors to women's PACs during the mid-1990s, Day and Hadley found that ELIST's donors in 1996 possessed consistently liberal policy positions on a wide range of issues, the most important issue being abortion (2005). Day and Hadley's study was based on a small non-random sample of ELIST donors.
3. Lorber (2005) provides a quick summary of feminisms on pages 26–27 and 63–64.
4. At the 2007 EMILY's List annual luncheon, Malcolm mentioned the need to secure women's reproductive rights, but only after she called for an end to the Iraq War, drew attention to the need for equal pay, and highlighted the work that female members of Congress were doing on important issues like healthcare and children's welfare. Personal experience at the EMILY's List's Annual Luncheon held at the Washington Convention Center, Washington, DC, March 6, 2007.
5. In fact, those concerned about low turnout rates have suggested that tax credits for political contributions (whether sent to a public financing system or to general candidates/parties/PACs) may increase Election Day turnout because individuals will then have a "stake" in the election outcome. This is discussed in depth in John M. de Figueiredo and Elizabeth Garrett's "Paying for Politics" (n.d.).
6. Big picture: Donor demographics (female donors). 2004. Open Secrets: Center for Responsive Politics. http://www.opensecrets.org/bigpicture/DonorDemographics.asp?Cycle=2004&filter=F (accessed May 15, 2009).

While this may be the case now, many scholars argue that the political system would benefit more from a more diverse donor pool. First, candidates would need to listen to different types of people and be less reliant on "special interests." Second, research indicates that those who donate money are more likely to participate in other ways. For these very reasons, some states have instituted tax credits or rebates for state-level candidates and other states have implemented a "clean money" system that provides public funding for state-level candidates. There is a study under way at the Campaign Finance Institute examining the behavior and political attitudes of donors in these states compared to donors in other states using data from the National Institute on Money in State Politics. 2009. http://www.followthemoney.org/index.phtml (accessed June 17, 2009).
7. Learn more about EMILY's List Majority Council. 2009. EMILY's List.http://emilyslist.org/support/majority_council/mc_learn_more/ (accessed on June 1, 2009).
8. See Barakso (2005) for a discussion of members influence on the National Organization of Women.
9. Since individuals who join EMILY's List cannot be easily labeled as donors or members, the following discussion refers to them as both: donors and members.
10. These data are from the detailed individual contributor file available for download at www.fec.gov.
11. Federal Election Commission campaign guide: Nonconnected committees. 2008. http://www.fec.gov/pdf/nongui.pdf. Federal Election Commission (accessed on June 1, 2009).
12. Since 2001, the FEC has allowed organizations to file electronically, which has led many organizations, including ELIST, to itemize their bundled contributions in amounts less than $200 rather than lump them together. Congressional Quarterly's Political Moneyline have these bundled data available and became the source for the bundled data from 2001–2008. However, because of the inconsistent quality of the data on smaller donations, it is not appropriate to use for a discussion of individual donor behavior.

13. These data only capture donors who gave $200 or more to EMILY's List during the 2000, 2002, 2004, 2006, and 2008 election cycles. CF scholars typically refer to these donors as "large" or "big" donors as opposed to donors who give less than $200, who are typically referred to as "small" donors.
14. Unlike Day and Hadley, these data are not survey-based but from FEC records and represents all EMILY's List members over an eight-year period. These differences in the sample and method allow for greater exploration of ELIST membership. Since I am interested in the entire universe of ELISTers, especially female donors, I used the entire universe of donors as my sample size instead of extracting an equal sample of male and female donors. While this is perfectly acceptable given my goals, any discussion or comparison of female and male donors must be must be viewed with circumspection. If nothing else, this study should highlight the need for a greater understanding of male ELISTers and intrigue scholars who are interested in comparing male and female political donors.
15. Personal communication with Joanne Howes, April 2008.
16. The ability of Francia et al. to discuss donor occupation is largely a function of their methodology—a survey of a sample of donors in which respondents were asked questions about their political behavior, political preferences, and basic demographic information, such as employer or occupation (current or former). The current study relies on data provided to the FEC by the organization, which was then recoded into standardized categories [see appendix B]. While ELIST is required to ask donors to report their employment/occupation, individuals do not always comply; thus, the quality of these data are sub-par. Still, it does provide some information about basic trends and allows for a basic comparison with these previous studies.
17. The donor occupation in the FEC records comes from the records of the PAC. When making a contribution to EMILY's List via their website using a credit card, donors must fill out certain information such as name, address, and occupation. These data go to the FEC via the organization's monthly reports. However, if a donor

leaves occupation blank OR simply sends EMILY's List a check, there is no way to determine his or her exact occupation unless it's listed on the check.
18. Francia et al. (2003) argued that the "none" occupational category should be understood as an attempt by the donors to "hide" their occupation as part of a bundling scheme or an attempt to circumvent limitations imposed first by FECA and more recently by the Bipartisan Campaign Reform Act of 2002 (BCRA) [discussed in chapters 2 and 3]. It is possible, however, that donors simply want to protect their occupation in the name of personal privacy rather than "nefarious" scheming.
19. This is a combination of financial, business sectors, and executive sectors.
20. My favorite entry is "parent of Chris, age 9."
21. In 2005, 51.2 percent of those employed in legal professions are women as compared to 48.8 percent in 2000. Data from the U.S. Census Bureau: http://factfinder.census.gov/servlet/QTTable?_bm=y&-geo_id=01000US&-qr_name=DEC_2000_SF3_U_QTP27&-ds_name=DEC_2000_SF3_U&-redoLog=false and http://factfinder.census.gov/servlet/STTable?_bm=y&-qr_name=ACS_2008_1YR_G00_S2401&-geo_id=01000US&-ds_name=ACS_2008_1YR_G00_&-_lang=en&-redoLog=false
22. It is important to note that these data contain a conservative estimate of EMILY's List's reach. It is quite possible that a significant percentage of smaller donors (those who give aggregate contributions of less than $200) live in other states, but data on these donors cannot be obtained from FEC records.
23. Only those states that provided EMILY's List with more than 300 members in a year are included in this table. Appendix C provides the raw number of donors for all states for each of the election cycles examined.
24. Office of Federal Relations: California congressional delegation roster, 111th Congress. 2009. The California State University. http://www.calstate.edu/FederalRelations/roster.shtml (accessed on May 1, 2009); Massachusetts congressional delegation: U.S. Senators. AllLaw.Com. http://www.alllaw.com/state_

resources/Massachusetts/congress/default.asp (accessed on June 1, 2009).
25. Although EMILY's List appeal *appears* to be stronger in these states, without further research it is impossible to determine whether this is due to EMILY's List activity (supporting candidates, direct mail, television ads, GOTV efforts) or a "friendly" political environment for female candidates, or whether it is simply an artifact of a higher population density and a higher per capita income. United States: State population estimates. 2008. U.S. Census Bureau. http://factfinder.census.gov/servlet/GCTTable?_bm=y&-geo_id=01000US&-_box_head_nbr=GCT-T1-R&-ds_name=PEP_2008_EST&-_lang=en&-format=US-40S&-_sse=on (accessed on June 1, 2009).
26. It is possible that this is a result of ELIST's targeting during midterms and the lack of any outside "noise" or "chatter" to distract potential members' attention, that is, ELIST members feel less torn and there are fewer competitors for their money during the midterm cycles.
27. See www.fec.gov. Independent expenditures are listed under "Committees or Candidates Supported or Opposed." Without tracing donor patterns over time, it is impossible to accurately determine the source of this difference; however, these data suggest that female and male ELISTers have been attracted to the organization at different times and at different rates. Further research is needed to fully flesh out these and other gender differences mentioned in previous sections.
28. A development executive at EMILY's List told Capeck that the organization's success in fundraising came from "...clear goals, a sense of community, and value-driven excitement..." (Capeck 1998, 24).
29. Another possible explanation for this decline is that individuals ideologically disposed to EMILY's List are already members. Thus, the most likely donor pool is smaller than in previous years, leading to a decline in new donors. This seems unlikely to have happened in 2008. A third possibility is that the donors classified as "new" large donors during this period are not truly "new" members but rather have given less than $200 in previous cycles and

thus did not show up in the FEC file. While this must be true to some degree, it cannot explain all of the new donors. Furthermore, this would likely occur in every election cycle, not just 2008.
30. As discussed in chapter 3, the organization has clout with the Democratic Party (insofar as the national party organization looks to EMILY's List to vet female candidates *and* the state parties partner with the organization to raise funds for GOTV) and with candidates, both potential (insofar as they would like to be an ELIST-endorsed candidate) and current (insofar as the organization has helped create a network of support for women with consultants, staffers, and so on, and the majority of Democratic women elected have received ELIST endorsement at some point in their career, if not multiple times).

CHAPTER 5

CANDIDATES AND THE ORGANIZATION

This chapter examines EMILY's List endorsements during the 2000–2008 election cycles. EMILY's List has escaped detailed attention by campaign finance scholars largely because it has been characterized as a traditional election-oriented PAC focused on challengers or open seat candidates via funding or recruitment. While that is part of EMILY's List's orientation, over the past twenty-five years, it has transformed itself into an organization that is much more than a PAC. To further elucidate the changes in EMILY's List, this chapter focuses on EMILY's List's endorsement strategy and how it relates to the organization's stated goals.

THE CHANGING DISTRIBUTION OF EMILY's LIST FUNDS

Data from the Center for American Women and Politics (CAWP) indicates that between 2000 and 2008, the number of Democratic women running for federal office steadily increased, but the number of candidates EMILY's List endorsed fluctuated, decreasing in 2000–2004, but rallying in 2006 and stabilizing in 2008 (see table 5.1). An examination of EMILY's List endorsements by seat status and chamber indicates that the change in the organization's strategy took place largely in their endorsement of House candidates during the 2000–2008 election cycles.

In the House, the decline occurs at all three levels, with some variation: the number of incumbent candidates supported declined from fourteen in 2000 to five in 2004, but rose to seven in 2008. The number of House challengers endorsed declined from thirteen in 2000 to six in 2004, but rose to twelve in 2008, and the number of open seat House candidates endorsed by EMILY's List declined from twelve in 2000 to five in 2004, rising to twelve in 2008. At the same time, ELIST's endorsement of Senate candidates remained stable until 2006, when the number of Senate candidates declined, only to rise again in 2008. In 2006 and 2008, the number of House candidates endorsed by the organization increased but the number of Senate candidates declined.

These data clearly show that the organization's endorsement decisions are strategic. In 2000 EMILY's List appeared to use more of a blanket strategy, supporting more candidates at all levels. In 2002 and 2004, the organization became more selective about endorsements. However, with majority control at stake in both the House and Senate in 2006 and 2008, the organization increased the sheer number of candidates endorsed and placed

TABLE 5.1. EMILY's List endorsement by seat status, chamber, and year, 2000–2008.

	Incumbents	Challengers	Open Seat	Total
2000				
U.S. House	14	13	12	39
U.S. Senate	1	4	1	6
Total	15	17	13	45
2002				
U.S. House	12	7	11	30
U.S. Senate	1	3	1	5
Total	13	10	12	35
2004				
U.S. House	5	6	5	16
U.S. Senate	3	1	3	7
Total	8	7	8	23
2006				
U.S. House	8	14	15	37
U.S. Senate	2	1	1	4
Total	10	15	16	41
2008				
U.S. House	7	19	12	38
U.S. Senate	0	2	0	2
Total	7	21	12	40

Source. Data from the Federal Election Commission.

more of its money and resources behind challengers and open seat candidates. Such a strategy suggests that the organization remains firmly committed to supporting challenger and open seat candidates, albeit fewer of them.

These data also make it clear that there are a variety of factors at work that affect EMILY's List's endorsement rates. It is also clear that EMILY's List is not a traditional access-oriented PAC. Whereas the previous chapters have explored ELIST's selective endorsement process and the role that viability plays, this chapter examines that process *empirically*.

Modeling EMILY's List Support

The empirical models tested in this chapter focus on two puzzles. First, why does EMILY's List choose to endorse some female Democratic candidates for Congress but not others? *Which Democratic women attract support from EMILY's List?* The second puzzle focuses on the period after an EMILY's List endorsement. What factors help explain why EMILY's List provides some endorsed candidates with large amounts and provides others with much less? *Which Democratic women attract extensive financial support from EMILY's List?* As with previous chapters, the focus herein is the congressional elections that occurred during the 2000–2008 period.

Data and Method

The data used in this chapter come from a variety of sources. The list of candidates comes from the Center on American Women and Politics (CAWP) and the Center for Responsive Politics (CRP). Data on the district or state, including presidential vote patterns (percent who supported the Democratic candidate in each election) and the final election results (vote percentage), come from several volumes of the *Almanac of American Politics*. Ratings of competitiveness come from rating reports by CQ Politics. Data pertaining to the total amount raised by candidates, first- and second-quarter funds, and all the data pertaining to EMILY's List activity on behalf of candidates come from the records of the FEC.[2]

Because the dependent variable (whether the organization endorses a candidate or not) is dichotomous, logistic regression provides the most appropriate method to examine why EMILY's List supports some female Democratic candidates but not others. OLS regression analysis is used to ascertain why the organization distributes large sums of PAC money to some women and less to others. Both sets of analyses focus on four factors: viability, incumbent status, competitiveness, and chamber.

As noted earlier, there is considerable belief among analysts that EMILY's List endorses only "serious" women candidates who have raised some considerable amount of money and have thereby demonstrated a base-level viability to their campaign. Thus, the first independent variable, viability, is used to measure a candidate's ability to raise money.

The second independent variable, whether the candidate ran as an incumbent, will illuminate whether EMILY's List concentrates its efforts on those running for reelection, who may be patrons and also may help protect the existing group of women in the Congress, or whether it focused on the election of non-incumbents who could help build the base of women in Congress.

A third independent variable is the competitiveness of the race. Has ELIST focused on helping women win in close races as an aggressive and concentrated way to solidify and increase women's presence in Congress, or has it utilized more of a blanket strategy? Competition is measured in two ways. The first is through the ratings of congressional races by Congressional Quarterly. The second measure is the percent of the vote the Democratic presidential candidate received in that particular district or state during the last presidential election. Districts or states where the Democratic presidential candidate received 55 percent or less in the general election are considered more competitive for Democrats.

The last independent variable is chamber. Is EMILY's List more concerned with supporting candidates in the House, the Senate, or a mixture of the two? In its effort to use its money to increase women in Congress, support for House candidates makes sense, since it costs less for House candidates to win than a Senate candidate. On the other hand, adding Democratic women to the Senate in some ways is more desirable, since the supermajoritarian sixty-vote nature of Senate policy-making gives women more potential leverage there. In addition, adding women to the Senate through the use of EMILY's List contributions could aid the visibility and power of EMILY's List more than helping to win House seats.

Who Does EMILY's List Endorse?

For each of the five election cycles examined, I perform a separate logistic regression on data for the universe of female Democratic candidates running in that year. The variables and coding schema for the logistic analyses are as follows:

Dependent variable:
- EMILY's List monetary support for the candidate[1] (1 = ELIST support; 0 = no ELIST support).

Independent variables:
- Dummy variable for seat status (1 = incumbent; 0 = other).
- First-quarter funds (in dollars): (1 = $0–$64; 2 = $65–$5,320; 3 = $5,321–$35,249; 4 = $35,250–$74,914; 5 = $74,915–$194,123; 6 = $194,124 and above).
- *Congressional Quarterly* rating for the race (1 = toss-up or lean Democrat or lean Republican; 0 = all others).
- Democratic vote for President in presidential election (percentage).
- Dummy variable for chamber (1 = House; 0 = Senate).

PREDICTING ELIST ENDORSEMENT

One might expect that as ELIST became more professional and powerful, the organization would become risk-averse in its endorsement of female Democratic candidates. Yet the organization has in some ways been *built* in reaction and opposition to risk aversion. Since its inception, EMILY's List and its members have targeted their efforts on electing the most viable female pro-choice Democratic candidates. It has not followed the "blanket" approach of other women's PACs discussed in chapter 2; just because a female candidate is pro-choice and Democratic does NOT mean she should expect *any* support from EMILY's List. Second, in the early years of EMILY's List, endorsed candidates were predominately challengers or open seat candidates who needed to prove to the gatekeepers of the more traditional sources of campaign money (the Democratic Party, Labor, etc.) that they were viable. However, in more recent years EMILY's List has endorsed an increasing number of female pro-choice Democratic incumbents.

While some may view this as risk-averse or a betrayal of the EMILY's List mission, the opposite is the case. If these female

Democratic incumbent candidates lose their seats, then the organization has *lost* the progress made in the past few decades. *Fulfilling ELIST's mission cannot occur by simply increasing the number of women in political office; that is only a first step.*

TABLE 5.2. Logistic regression: Who is EMILY's List more likely to support?

	2000	2002	2004	2006	2008
Democratic Party Support	7.399**	2.367	6.790*	23.2***	7.629**
	(.706)	(.560)	(.854)	(.769)	(.650)
Competition	.852	2.911	10.052*	3.119	2.744
	(.582)	(.619)	(.927)	(.645)	(.560)
First Quarter	1.780***	1.568**	2.650***	2.586***	2.169***
	(.170)	(.147)	(.267)	(.196)	(.188)
Chamber	.365	1.161	.073*	1.011	3.495
	(.968)	(.754)	(1.148)	(1.059)	(1.266)
Incumbency	.327*	.462	.224	.057***	.038***
	(.558)	(.554)	(.894)	(.875)	(.727)
Constant	.084*	.002	.015	.006***	.004***
	(1.071)	(.943)	(1.541)	(1.353)	(1.541)
N	115	124	137	157	159
−2 LL	110.237	123.667	68.573	97.806	112.652
Chi-square	43.708	22.005	55.235	84.556	66.718
p-value	.000	.000	.000	.000	.000

Note. Dependent variable is EMILY's List endorsement, with 1=yes and 0=no.
*** significant at p<.001 level; ** significant at p<.01; *significant at p<.05 level.

An examination of the role competition played in EMILY's List endorsement decisions indicates that competition (i.e., a candidate running in a race designated as a "turnover" or "leaning" seat) only significantly affected the odds of an ELIST endorsement in 2004. In that cycle, female Democratic candidates running in competitive races were 10.05 times more likely to receive an ELIST endorsement than those running in less competitive races. Why is 2004 different than the other election cycles? In 2004 the organization endorsed a *greater number* of candidates in highly competitive races, likely due to the Democratic Party's loss of nine congressional seats in 2002 (eight seats in the House and one in the Senate) (Mann, Ornstein, and Malbin 2008, 54). It is also in 2004 that chamber becomes a significant predictor of the organization's endorsement decision. Female Democrats engaged in a House campaign in 2004 were slightly more likely to be endorsed by the organization than those running for a Senate seat.

In all five elections, incumbents were slightly more likely than challengers and open seat candidates to receive an EMILY's List endorsement. This is expected, as EMILY's List does not want female Democratic candidates who have already made it into office to lose their seats and any power/influence they have acquired. Yet it is important to note that the power of incumbency vis-à-vis capturing an ELIST endorsement is consistent across cycles. In 2006 and 2008, incumbency is a *very significant* predictor of endorsement, a fact explained by political contextual factors. Both 2006 and 2008 were highly competitive elections. In 2006 the Democratic Party gained back control of the House for the first time in twelve years; key to this strategy was the protection of vulnerable incumbents. In 2008 the GOP sought to regain control of the House and simultaneously prevent the Democrats from obtaining a supermajority in the Senate. Once again, considerable effort went into targeting vulnerable incumbents, which had party adjuncts such as EMILY's List closing ranks to protect the gains made in earlier years.

While competition, chamber, and seat status provide insight into differences in ELIST's endorsement strategy during the 2000–2008 period, the best predictors of an ELIST endorsement are the partisanship of the state/district and the candidate's ability to raise money.

Democratic Areas

Candidates running in states/districts where voters provided more support to the Democratic presidential candidate during the last presidential election were more likely to be endorsed by the organization. The power of this predictor varied significantly during the period. During presidential cycles (2000, 2004, and 2008), candidates from areas with greater levels of Democratic support were 6.8 to 7.6 times more likely to receive an endorsement by the organization. In 2006 those in Democratic areas were 23 times more likely to receive an endorsement than those in less Democratic areas. In 2002 the level of Democratic support in the district/state did not achieve statistical significance.

First-Quarter Receipts

It should come as no surprise, given the discussion of ELIST's origins and growth in previous chapters, that viability measured via first-quarter receipts constitute a highly significant predictor of an ELIST endorsement in all of the election cycles examined. In 2000 and 2002, candidates who raised more money in the first quarter were between 1.58 and 1.78 times more likely to receive an ELIST endorsement than those who raised less money. The explanatory power of this variable increased during the period. In 2000 candidates with higher first-quarter receipts were 1.7

times more likely to be endorsed by EMILY's List; in 2008, the odds increased to 2.2.

These models provide definitive evidence of two important things. First, they provide an empirically based model for the organization's endorsement process. While the organization has remained relatively steadfast in its explanation of who it endorses—a candidate must be: 1) pro-ERA/pro-choice/progressive; 2) female; 3) a Democrat; and 4) viable—the way the organization defines or interprets these criteria has not been established empirically. This lack of empirical evidence would not matter as much if the organization was more definite about the factors that influence its decisions and/or if the organization had less influence in congressional elections. But EMILY's List *is* influential, and this model indicates that the ability of a candidate to raise money is critical to a candidate's chances. Second, political context *matters a great deal* to the EMILY's List endorsement process. In cycles where there are a number of vulnerable incumbents or if majority control of Congress is at stake, EMILY's List will adjust its decision-making process to reflect these political realities.

WHO GETS MORE DOUGH?

EMILY's List's decision to support or not support a female Democratic congressional candidate is only part of the story. The other part is how much support the organization provides candidates. It is possible that one set of considerations dominates the decision to endorse women candidates, whereas another set of considerations dominates the decision to give some endorsed candidates large amounts of money and other women less. To determine whether the organization approaches its decisions about how much money to give candidates in a different manner from its decision to endorse candidates, I have performed a series of linear regressions on the level of EMILY's List contributions to all female Democratic congressional candidates between 2000 and 2008. The variables in these regression analyses are listed below:

Dependent variable:
- Total amount of EMILY's List funding (in dollars).

Independent variables:
- Dummy variable for seat status (1 = incumbent; 0 = other).
- First-quarter funds (in dollars): (1 = $0–$64; 2 = $65–$5,320; 3 = $5,321–$35,249; 4 = $35,250–$74,914; 5 = $74,915–$194,123; 6 = $194,124 and above).
- *Congressional Quarterly* rating (1 = toss-up or lean Democratic or lean Republican; 0 = other).
- Democratic vote for President in presidential election (percentage).
- Dummy variable for chamber (1 = House; 0 = Senate).

Results

The models of endorsement indicate that EMILY's List and its membership were strategic in which endorsed candidates received the most financial help from ELIST and its members, ELIST's strategic use of resources becomes apparent once again. In 2000, 2004, and 2006, competition is a significant predictor of how much money an endorsed candidate received (see table 5.3). In fact, in 2000 and 2006, competition is the *only* significant predictor in the model. Endorsed candidates who ran in highly competitive seats (those designated as "turnover" or "leaning") received more money than those in less competitive seats.

Candidates and the Organization

TABLE 5.3. Predicting EMILY's List dollars.

	2000	2002	2004	2006	2008
Democratic Party Support	.047	.035	−.266	.055	.241
Competition	.420**	.141	.424*	.502**	.261
Chamber	−.220	.412*	−.578**	−.252	−.279*
Incumbency	−.233	−.539**	−.120	−.203	−.211
First-Quarter Receipts	.233	.736**	.077	−.212	.182
R^2	.562	.534	.496	.441	.370
p-value	.000	.000	.027	.001	.006

Note. Dependent variable is the amount of money (in dollars) EMILY's List provides to candidate (bundled and direct/in-direct contribution). R^2 is not adjusted because these data are for the entire population under study. OLS regression coefficients; *** significant at p<.001 level; ** significant at p<.01; *significant at p<.05 level.

In 2004 chamber is also a statistically significant predictor of how much financial help a candidate received from ELIST. Not only did candidates in highly competitive races receive significantly higher amounts of money from ELIST, but endorsed candidates who ran for the U.S. Senate also receive significantly higher levels of support.

On its face, this is unsurprising—Senate races are *far* more costly than House races—but if we follow that logic, why isn't chamber always significant? Furthermore, the relationship between chamber and the amount of money a candidate receives from ELIST is not always as expected. In 2002 the relationship is significant but in the opposite direction. In that cycle, endorsed candidates who ran in House races received higher levels of money from ELIST and its membership than those who ran for the Senate. Furthermore, incumbency and first-quarter receipts were significant predictors of the level of support a candidate received from ELIST in 2002, but *only* in that cycle.

In every other election cycle examined—2000, 2004, 2006, and 2008—ELIST's distributive decision making appears fluid. In 2000 and 2006, only competition emerged as a statistically significant predictor of the level of financial support an endorsed candidate received from ELIST and its members. As expected, those in more competitive races received a higher level of money. In 2004 competition and chamber were significant; female Democratic women endorsed by ELIST and running in competitive Senate races received a higher level of financial support from the organization and its members. In 2008 the relationship between the level of money and chamber was negative and statistically significant; those running for a Senate seat received significantly higher levels of funds.

These findings are incredibly important, as they illuminate the ability and the willingness of ELIST and its membership to adjust *how much* they financially support a candidate based on the political context of any cycle. It is this keen political acumen that members trust—that is why receipts to EMILY's List continue to grow—and it helps explain how this organization has become a political powerhouse. From its inception, Malcolm pursued a slow piecemeal approach to EMILY's List expansion, and that includes its endorsement strategy. Her goal—and the goal of ELIST members who provide over $25 million a year to the organization and its candidates—was a long-term one. While individual races and individual election cycles matter, the focus of the organization remains the larger mission: to elect pro-choice Democratic women to office so that they can acquire the political power necessary to change public policy and potentially our political institutions.

For these reasons, one should not be surprised by the fluidity of endorsement and distribution strategy. Fluidity helped the organization marshal its resources in a way that allowed it to meet its multiple goals: 1) electing pro-ERA/pro-choice/progressive Democratic women to all levels of political office; 2) creating and sustaining a progressive majority in government; and 3) mobilizing progressive men and women actors across the country to fund, elect, and reelect these candidates.[3]

CONCLUSION

The evidence provided in this chapter demonstrates that EMILY's List's status as a PAC is not determinative of its actions. If the organization was a simple, traditional election-oriented PAC, it would have focused all of its money and resources on challenger and open seat candidates who are ideologically representative of the organization's policy preferences. While it continued to endorse a number of women and give some funds to these women irrespective of their competitiveness or incumbency status, it increasingly used the bulk of its funds in a more focused and concentrated manner, focusing on a small number of women in competitive races. In so doing, EMILY's List focused on trying to make a *critical difference* in a few races in order to both increase the number of women in Congress and help increase the margin of Democratic seats to affect majority control of the institution.

In sum, EMILY's List responded in some dramatic ways to changes in its environment and in its own effectiveness over the past decade or so. When few women were in Congress and the real issue was building a broad base of women candidates to compete for office, EMILY's List endorsed a larger number of women, spread its money widely, and aggressively pushed Democratic pro-choice women as a group forward. But as women have increasingly gained seats in Congress and as incumbent women have many sources to draw on for campaign funds, the organization has changed its strategy. In part, as discussed earlier, the organization on supporting candidates in state- and local-level races. But it has also changed the nature of its congressional strategy. Particularly in light of the close margins between Democrats and Republicans in Congress and the particular value of additional women in the Senate during the 2000–2008 period, EMILY's List focused on trying to distribute major funds to a small number of women in competitive races where victory could both increase the number of women on the Hill and affect congressional control.

In the process, EMILY's List evolved in ways quite different from traditional PACs that highlight the fact that, while being a PAC, it is much more than a PAC. It is a multipronged influence organization that seeks to increase women's actual influence on the Hill. Its strategy for accomplishing that is to increase the number of Democratic women elected to Congress, thus increasing the chance that such women will have access to power by being members of the majority party. As Malcolm stated in her endorsement of Hillary Clinton's presidential campaign, "In 1988, when EMILY's List began supporting congressional candidates, there were only 12 Democratic women in the House. Now Nancy Pelosi is the first woman Speaker in U.S. history—a feat made possible, in part, because of the support she has among the 50 Democratic women who serve in the House today" (Malcolm 2007). Whereas traditional PACs tend to increasingly focus on giving to safe incumbents as a way to gain access to patrons, EMILY'S List has increasingly focused its attention and resources in a way that positions Democratic pro-choice women *as a group* with access to political power.

Today, to receive EMILY's List support a woman must be Democratic, pro-choice, and serious about running. But to receive extensive funds, these women must generally be non-incumbents in competitive races whose election can make a real difference in the power of women on Capitol Hill. This strategy is a reasonable and realistic one, precisely because EMILY's List and other women's organizations proved so successful in the 1980s and 1990s in fostering women Democratic candidates for Congress and aiding them in winning seats so that Democratic women would increasingly attain power in Congress.

Endnotes

1. ELIST support includes any money given to the candidate via a direct or in-direct contribution or a bundled contribution from the organization's members.
2. Following the procedure established by Francia (2001), "first-quarter receipts" is the total amount raised by a candidate in the first quarter after he or she officially files as a candidate. This procedure helps control for the fact that some candidates announce their candidacy immediately in the election cycle, whereas others may not enter until mere months before the primary.
3. Although ELIST's goal is to elect women, they have always provided some support to progressive male Democratic candidates. The amount of this support has grown over the years. Specific data are available through the records of the Federal Election Commission at www.fec.gov.

Chapter 6

EMILY's List and Its "Mojo"

The focus of this chapter is the 2008 election, specifically EMILY's List's entrée into presidential politics and what that meant for the organization, its mission, its leadership, its members, and its future. From the beginning, EMILY's List's mission has been to help elect viable pro-choice Democratic female candidates into elected office. Thus, the organization's endorsement of Hillary Clinton's presidential campaign should not have come as a surprise to anyone. Clinton clearly met all the criteria for an EMILY's List endorsement: she could raise considerable money, had a top-notch campaign team, was considered viable, and had a long history of supporting the tenets of *Roe v. Wade* (1973). However, the organization's participation in the 2008 presidential campaign and, more specifically, the battle over the Democratic Party nomination left many concerned about its fate.

Democratic Women and the White House

From 1985 until 2007, two women sought the Democratic nomination for President: Pat Schroeder (1988) and Carol Mosley Braun (2004). EMILY's List did not endorse either. According to the Center for American Women and Politics (CAWP), Schroeder "took preliminary steps toward making a serious run for the presidency, but dropped out before the primaries because she could not raise the necessary funds" (Center for American Women and Politics 2008). In the case of Braun, EMILY's List had played a key role in her successful 1992 Senate campaign; her election as the first African-American woman elected to the Senate was a monumental victory and figures prominently in the organization's success stories (EMILY's List n.d.[c]). When she came up for reelection in 1998, the organization provided her with $5,000 via a direct contribution from its PAC. However, Braun lost her race. According to National Public Radio:

> If there was tremendous promise in Carol Moseley Braun's career in 1992, it had very much dissipated by 1998. There was a sense that she had squandered a tremendous opportunity. For starters, she was accused of (though never formally charged with) campaign finance irregularities, her then-fiancé (and campaign manager) was accused of sexual harassment by female campaign workers, and her "private" trip to Nigeria in 1996, where she visited with and defended dictator Sani Abacha, was widely panned, even by many Democrats. Considerably outspent, she lost her bid for re-election in 1998, the only Democratic incumbent to be ousted that year, and the first Illinois Democrat to lose a Senate race in 20 years.[1]

When Braun decided to run for the Democratic Party nomination for President in 2004, she sought EMILY's List support. Braun pled her case to a group of EMILY's List delegates:

> While the applause for Braun was vigorous, she did not receive a standing ovation from the women's group, as Kucinich did. The group emphasizes supporting women candidates, but officials said they are so intent on defeating President Bush that they are searching for the nominee who stands the best chance of being elected. "We are looking at their viability," said Janet Harris, a spokeswoman for EMILY's List. (Zeleny 2003)

Ultimately, the PAC decided that person was not Braun. EMILY's List did not give her any direct or in-kind contributions or bundled money, nor did it spend any money on independent expenditures to support her candidacy.[2] Braun ultimately withdrew from the race due to problems raising money (National Public Radio 2004).

Even though the organization did not endorse Schroeder or Braun, EMILY's List and its leadership had been active in prior presidential elections. Before the creation of ELIST, many of the Founding Mothers of EMILY's List played a key role in the 1984 presidential campaign. Some reportedly put considerable pressure on Walter Mondale to choose a woman as his vice-presidential running mate, and most, if not all, were active in Geraldine Ferraro's vice-presidential campaign.[3] In fact Mondale and Ferraro's loss in 1984, especially the treatment that Ferraro received, is one of the impetuses behind EMILY's List's formation. More recently, the organization spent more than $90,000 on independent expenditures in support of the Democratic candidate John Kerry and over $5,000 in opposition to George W. Bush, not to mention the money spent on voter mobilization through its WOMEN VOTE! program in several battleground states (EMILY's List n.d.[a]). Furthermore, the organization's former executive director, Mary Beth Cahill, served as campaign manager for the Kerry campaign.

Divisions: The Parties and the Candidates

The minor role that ELIST played in the 2004 presidential campaign paled in comparison to its role in the 2008 presidential campaign. As mentioned in chapter 1, just hours after Clinton's announcement that she was officially running for the Democratic nomination for President of the United States, EMILY's List endorsed her. It is possible that those who considered the organization simply a women's PAC did not find the EMILY's List endorsement of Clinton remarkable; insofar as women's PACs exist to support female candidates, the organization's behavior would raise few eyebrows. However, for those who looked to the organization as a proxy for the Democratic Party, EMILY's List's immediate endorsement of Clinton was a shot across the bow. The partisan stakes in 2008 were no less dire than those in 2004. Hadn't the organization set aside gender for the good of the Democratic Party then? Why not now?

Anyone who questioned EMILY's List's endorsement of Clinton lacked a clear understanding of the organization's multifaceted nature and its strategic leadership. Evidence indicates that in 2004, the organization based its decision on viability and partisanship, not on identity concerns. Why should it support a candidate who would surely lose? But in January 2007, few questioned Clinton's viability. This time the gendered aspect of the organization's mission—to elect pro-choice Democratic women to public office—did not have to be put aside to focus on its partisan mission.

In some ways, the role of EMILY's List in the battle for the 2008 Democratic presidential nomination was simply the latest and the most public example of the organization's refusal to back down. As far back as 1992, the organization stood its ground against the Democratic Party establishment if there was a viable pro-choice Democratic female candidate who had as good a chance of winning as the Party's male candidate.[4] While the rivalry between EMILY's List and some of the Democratic Party leadership may have been seen as routine or gone largely unnoticed by members and the media in the past, in 2008 it became part of the main story.

As the battle for the Democratic presidential nomination raged, ELIST also faced conflict within the organization. The 2008 election cycle marked only the second time that the organization had been forced to address the fact that the candidates it helped elect had beliefs and constituencies that could be very different than those of the organization. The first conflict between ELIST and its candidates occurred in the late 1990s when two EMILY's List–endorsed candidates, Senator Mary Landrieu (D-LA) and Senator Blanche Lincoln (D-AR), voted in support of the Partial Birth Abortion Ban. Malcolm issued a public response to the votes: "Since these senators no longer meet EMILY's List's criteria on choice, they will be removed from the EMILY's List advisory committee and will no longer be eligible for EMILY's List support" (National Right to Life News 2001; McClusky 2009; Jewell 2003).

But the attention Malcolm's displeasure received in 1999 was minimal compared to that accompanying Senator Claire McCaskill's (D-MO) public endorsement of Obama in January 2008. McCaskill, one of EMILY's List's superstar candidates in 2006, made the announcement a mere four days after Clinton's upset victory in the New Hampshire primary, in which ELIST played a significant role (Overby 2007). In her announcement, Senator McCaskill stated, "I have deep respect for Hillary Clinton. She is a smart woman. She is a strong leader. But at this moment in history, it is very important that we look forward with a kind of optimism and hope" (McCormick 2008).

According to one source, McCaskill actually supported Obama's candidacy long before her announcement "but had been reluctant to step forward earlier out of loyalty to Emily's List" and "had faced strong pressure from her women's group allies to support the former first lady, or at least stay neutral" (Murray 2008). Ultimately, McCaskill claimed that her daughter convinced her to come out publicly for Obama. "She was a loose brick in what had been expected to be a solid Democratic wall of support for Clinton from her female colleagues. Here was a senator from a key swing state whose own success had been fueled by votes and money from women—whose mother had been the first woman elected to the Columbia, MO, city council—and she was rejecting the first woman who had a good chance of becoming president" (Goldstein 2008).

The Membership Reacts

The conflict between the organization and several of its candidates became a proxy for the conflict among women and between women and men regarding Clinton's candidacy (Vaida and Skalka 2008). As discussed in chapter 4, donors to EMILY's List are largely female and the organization has historically had a membership that tends to be older and white (Day and Hadley 2005). From all accounts, those EMILY's List members who were older white women were unfazed if not ecstatic by the organization's decision to endorse Clinton. Members immediately sent bundled checks to Clinton through EMILY's List and sent separate contributions to the PAC to ensure that both ELIST and Clinton had the necessary resources to win. All told, EMILY's List bundled just over $855,000 to Clinton's campaign from its members. Using receipts from the PAC and its 527, in late December, EMILY's List launched the WOMEN VOTE! program in New Hampshire, targeting 50,000 Democratic women voters. A few weeks later, New Hampshire gave Clinton her first victory; she had lost the Iowa caucuses just a few days prior. On the heels of Clinton's victory in New Hampshire, EMILY's List deployed the WOMEN VOTE! program in New Jersey and Connecticut, using targeted mail and phone banks to contact more than 87,000 female voters in those states. Between March and May, the organization, working in its campaign organization capacity, used the WOMEN VOTE! program to target likely female Democratic voters in Ohio, Texas, Pennsylvania, and Virginia (EMILY's List 2008c).

EMILY's List Chastises Colleagues

Having functioned largely as a PAC and a campaign organization in 2007 and early 2008, the organization took on its interest-group function in mid-May 2008, when the National Abortion Rights Action League (NARAL)—one of the leading interest groups working on protecting women's right to choose—publicly endorsed Senator Obama. Malcolm, who had not issued a statement when McCaskill made her announcement, immediately issued a statement:

> I think it is tremendously disrespectful to Sen. Clinton—who held up the nomination of a FDA commissioner in order to force approval of Plan B and who spoke so eloquently during the Supreme Court nomination about the importance of protecting *Roe vs. Wade*—to not give her

the courtesy to finish the final three weeks of the primary process. It certainly must be disconcerting for elected leaders who stand up for reproductive rights and expect the choice community will stand with them. (Malcolm 2008)

EMILY's List is often kept from working in coalition with other women's interest groups because of its partisan mission. However, given that ELIST and many other feminist women's organizations share the goal of protecting a woman's right to choose, and because that is EMILY's List's singular explicit policy goal, contention is rare. For example, ELIST and NARAL might work together to support (or oppose) certain candidates for the Supreme Court. But unlike NARAL, whose activity and mission is centered on achieving its policy goals, ELIST's interest-group function and its goal of protecting *Roe v. Wade* (1973) is not a zero-sum game. Since it is a multipronged influence organization, the organization's leadership is ever cognizant of the need to balance the goals and activities of one prong against those of the others. Some might argue that in its endorsement of Clinton, the organization's leadership decided to sacrifice its partisan goals for its gendered mission. However, in evaluating the organization's status in the aftermath of the 2008 election, it is difficult to identify areas of significant loss to any aspect of the organization.

EMILY's List: Resilient or Wrecked?

In terms of the organization's PAC activities, during 2008, the organization brought in more money than ever ($35.2 million, up from $34.1 in 2006)—although according to FEC records the amount of receipts from individuals declined slightly ($24.9 million in 2006 to $23.4 million in 2008).[5] The organization provided its candidates with over $244,951 in direct and in-direct contributions. It conducted two separate waves of WOMEN VOTE! programs, one during the Democratic primary and one in the last month of the general election. The microtargeting data available in the 2008 edition of the *Women's Monitor*, which focused on the similarities and differences among women "From 18 to 80," informed the organization's efforts to mobilize voters through WOMEN VOTE! (*Women's Monitor* 2008). The *Monitor* and the additional polling also helped it fulfill EMILY's List's role as a Democratic Party adjunct by bringing disaffected Clinton supporters back to the fold after Barack Obama's victory in the Democratic primary (EMILY's List 2008b).

There are only a few indications that EMILY's List's efforts to help Clinton cinch the Democratic nomination caused the organization any hardship. According to FEC records, in 2008, the organization ended the cycle with more than $900,000 in debt. In the organization's twenty-five year history, this is only the second time EMILY's List ended an election cycle in debt, the first occurring in 2006. It is possible that the organization's expanded scope in 2006 and 2008—fighting both partisan and gender battles on all three levels of our electoral system—strained its resources. However, with four endorsements for the 2010 midterms announced by March 2009, there is little evidence of the organization retreating.

There is some evidence that the organization's membership suffered a few pangs during the 2008 election cycle beyond the slight decline in individual receipts. As discussed in chapter 4, in 2008, the percentage of new donors to the organization declined from 47 percent in 2006 to 31.6 percent in 2008. The decline could be the result of several factors; its increased appeals to those seeking partisan and not necessarily gender gains could create a more unstable membership, especially in times of conflict between the organization and the Democratic Party. The percentage of men giving large donations to the organization also decline slightly, from 26.8 percent in 2006 to 21.2 percent in 2008. It is possible these declines were the result of ELIST's involvement in the Democratic primary. However, the declines could also be reflective of the more general trend of a lower numbers of new members in presidential cycles.[6]

Conclusion

As the primary campaign ended and Clinton withdrew from the presidential race, some wondered if this signaled the organization's decline. The July 2009 cover of the *National Journal* featured Ellen Malcolm; the title asked, "Can Emily's List Get Its Mojo Back?" (Vaida and Skalka 2008). If ELIST was just a women's PAC and it had bet all of its resources on Clinton's candidacy, then such concern would have been appropriate. While Malcolm acknowledged the differences between ELIST's current membership base and its future membership base of current "post-feminist" twenty-somethings, she remained pragmatic:

> People who are donors to politics across the board are older, because they have the wherewithal to do it. Am I going to craft a message for 18-year-olds right now and try to raise money from them? No. (Vaida and Skalka 2008)

As an entrepreneurial leader who transformed a donor network comprised of a small group of well-connected female politicos into a multipronged influence organization with over 100,000 members nationwide, Malcolm is neither naive nor shortsighted. Immediately after the end of the Democratic primary, ELIST endorsed Senator Barack Obama as the Democratic nominee and Malcolm deployed the organization's considerable resources to help ensure a Democratic victory in November. From its inception, Malcolm and others knew that EMILY's List was not a short-term project but rather one that required political opportunity and persistence.

In the end, although the 2008 presidential election did not bring the election of Hillary Clinton as the first female President of the United States, it did bring more than one ELISTer into the White House. On November 22, 2008, the executive director, Ellen Moran, stepped down from EMILY's List to become the communications director for the White House and in January 2009 Hillary Rodham Clinton was sworn in as U.S. Secretary of State.

ENDNOTES

1. National Public Radio interview with Former Sen. Carol Moseley Braun. 2003. National Public Radio. http://www.npr.org/programs/specials/democrats2004/braun.html (accessed on June 1, 2009).
2. Committees and candidates supported/opposed (EMILY's List). 2003. Federal Election Commission. http://query.nictusa.com/cgi-bin/com_supopp/2003_C00193433 (accessed on June 1, 2009).
3. Clift and Brazaitas (2003); personal communication with Joanne Howes, April 2008; personal communication with Judith Lichtman, June 2008.
4. Personal communication with Ramona Oliver of EMILY's List, April 2008.
5. See www.fec.gov.
6. The data in chapter 4 indicate that ELIST draws in fewer new donors in presidential years than in midterm cycles. When contacted for an interview in April 2008, both Ellen Malcolm and Judith Lichtman were traveling the country in support of Clinton's candidacy. It would be difficult to find out why individuals did not join the organization in 2008. The closest way to measure the reasons behind new donor decline may be to conduct a survey of members who gave to the organization in earlier cycles but did not give in 2008.

CHAPTER 7

CONCLUSION

In November 2006, EMILY's List and its membership rejoiced as the Democrats took control of Congress; soon thereafter, Nancy Pelosi was elected the first female Speaker of the House. This change in party control brought changes in congressional leadership: four Democratic women became chair of House committees and EMILY's List's first executive director, Rosa DeLauro (CT-3), became one of the top Democratic leaders in the House.[1] In the Senate, Senator Barbara Boxer (D-CA) became chair of the Environment and Public Works Committee and Senator Dianne Feinstein (D-CA) became chair of the Rules and Administration Committee.

Just two months later, Senator Hillary Rodham Clinton (D-NY) announced that she would be running for the office of President of the United States. EMILY's List endorsed her that same day and put the full weight of the organization and its resources toward that goal. Although the outcome was not what the organization had hoped, in January of 2007, the presidential inauguration of Barack Obama and the swearing in of Hillary Rodham Clinton as U.S. Secretary of State brought its own joy. That feeling was deepened by the knowledge that all but two of the seventy-nine Democratic women sworn in as members of the 111th Congress were women that EMILY's List helped elect.[2]

Yet even though its impact is apparent, little systematic research has been done on this organization. The goal of this book is to illuminate the organization's impact by examining its roots in the women's movement, its place within the world of campaign finance, its efforts to get pro-choice Democratic women into office, its impact on the mobilization and participation of the mass public (especially women), and its relationship with the Democratic Party. In exploring EMILY's List in these ways, this book contains a series of important findings.

One of the earliest questions asked in this project was, to what extent is EMILY's List simply a very successful women's PAC and to what extent is it something more? In comparing the organization to other women's PACs, it quickly became apparent that EMILY's List is *much* different than other women's PACs. By 1992, its influence and impact quickly superseded the others. Little is gained by looking at the organization as a women's PAC in 1992 and beyond; much more can be learned by viewing it as a multipronged influence organization that simultaneously functions as a PAC, an interest group, a campaign organization, and a party adjunct.

LEADERS AND MEMBERS

As detailed in chapter 2, Ellen Malcolm learned from watching Labor and others navigate the waters of the PAC world and negotiate the political and legal juggernaut that is campaign finance. Perhaps most importantly, she realized the need to make EMILY's List into a reference group for its members. Souraf (1992) claimed that Labor's ability to become a symbol and a shortcut for its members helps explain its longevity and power. This is part of the secret to EMILY's List success as well. Malcolm used a certain type of identity politics to connect the organization to the women's movement. In the early years of the organization, the successes and failures of the liberal feminist women's movement helped fuel donor passions; in 1992, the embers Malcolm had been fanning burst into flame, helped along by serendipitous events like the retirement of several incumbents and redistricting. They have remained burning brightly ever since.

Critical to the organization's post-1992 successes was its expansion into new arenas like mobilizing women voters, training campaign professionals, and recruiting and training candidates. As discussed in chapters 3 and 4, these efforts paid off handsomely for the organization, boosting the membership from 23,000 in 1992 to over 100,000 in 2008.

But not all members are the same, nor do they all receive the same benefits. Using FEC records, it appears that only a small percentage of EMILY's List members give the organization their "promised" dues of $200/year. Still, the large percentage of small donors, or free riders (Olson 1965), does not hinder the organization's power. In fact, in some ways it actually strengthens EMILY's List's claim of grassroots organizing, of reaching out to help people, especially women, find their voice and their checkbook (EMILY's List n.d.[b]). This is echoed in the organization's ability to pull in a significant amount of new members each cycle. For the most part, these new donors are women, which flies in the face of the persistent gender gap in political donations.

How has EMILY's List been able to consistently grow when others have wavered? Part of the answer is that Malcolm continues to use identity-driven appeals (presented in the organization's mailings) to keep members cognizant of the need for women in political office and focused on the accomplishments of the women who have made it. Furthermore, the organization adheres to a strict hierarchical structure. While there are divisions within the organization (different branches, regional directors, etc.), as well as a number of individuals in senior-level leadership positions, from all accounts Malcolm firmly steers the organization and has the final word on all decisions. Her entrepreneurial leadership and strategic vision help to explain how EMILY's List has been able to take advantage of political opportunities and adapt to changing political environments.

CANDIDATES AND ELECTIONS

The other way to explain EMILY's List's unstoppable rise to power is the candidates it supports. When first learning of EMILY's List and its small beginnings—endorsing only two candidates in 1986, only one of whom (Mikulski) won—one might wrongly assume that the organization started small because it lacked funds or lacked candidates. After hearing that the organization now brings in upward of $35 million in receipts each cycle, one might assume that it gives equal support to every pro-choice female Democratic candidate running for office. This is not the case. Left out of this scenario is *the* critical element in the organization's endorsement criteria: viability. The two women EMILY's List endorsed in 1986 were not the only female pro-choice Democrats on the ballot—but they were the only two Malcolm and the other Founding Mothers thought could win if only they had the resources. The same type of calculation is at work today, though it occurs on a much larger scale and involves many more people all over the country.

Measuring the organization's influence is also more difficult now that it has gone from a donor PAC to a multipronged influence organization. Whereas the organization's influence on a candidate's campaign was relatively easy to trace from 1986–1992 by tracking bundled money and the direct and in-direct contributions of the PAC through FEC records, after the organization expanded its repertoire of services (discussed in chapter 3), measuring its impact and influence is much more difficult. To *fully* measure the organization's impact on a campaign, one would not only have to capture the bundled checks and direct and in-kind contributions but also the money spent on independent expenditures, funds spent on training the candidate and her campaign staff (which likely occurred at least one cycle before the current race), money spent on GOTV efforts to mobilize voters in her district/state, money spent on training any Campaign Corps volunteer assigned to the campaign (if applicable), a portion of the costs associated with the data collection used in microtargeting (*Women's Monitor*), and a portion of the salary of the staff devoted to identifying and tracking the candidate and the campaign throughout the race.

Without accurate measures of how much the organization is spending on the races of its endorsed candidates, it is impossible to fully assess its full impact on election outcomes. Consequently, the empirical models in chapter 5 focus on who EMILY's List chooses to endorse and which endorsed candidates get the most money from the PAC and its members. Over the course of twenty-five years, the organization *has* become more strategic about *which* pro-choice Democratic women receive support. EMILY's List allocates money to its candidates depending on a variety of factors; the ability to raise money, the competitiveness of the district/state, and the characteristics of the seat can all play a role. Pro-choice female Democratic candidates who are able to raise money and are running in competitive districts have the best odds of an EMILY's List endorsement.

In terms of EMILY's List's state-level program, it is clear that the organization is spending a considerable amount to recruit and train women at the state and local levels, not to mention bundling money and giving direct and in-direct contributions.[3] While EMILY's List has become more strategic in its endorsements of federal candidates, it did not abandon its original mission: to make women equal players in American political institutions. The organization recognized the necessity of supporting women at lower levels and has allocated an increasingly significant amount of its resources toward that endeavor.

THE EMILY's LIST MODEL:
A MULTIPRONGED INFLUENCE ORGANIZATION

EMILY's List: The PAC

Is EMILY's List a women's PAC? Yes, insofar as it is a PAC created by women to support women candidates. Given its beginning as a women's PAC and its continued PAC activity—bundling money and giving direct and in-kind contributions—it is not surprising that many still view it through that lens. However, we miss a great deal by limiting our perspective in this way. For example, scholars tend to assess the influence of PACs according to how much money they give to candidates; historically, PACs have been viewed as vehicles used to buy access to candidates. EMILY's List, however, does not give a large percentage of their receipts or disbursements to candidates because: 1) they are a non-connected PAC, and as such, all of their overhead expenses must be paid out of receipts; 2) they focus on bundling money to candidates; and 3) ELIST does *other* things that are not typically included in scholars' assessments of PAC power.

Classifying EMILY's List as just a women's PAC places it in a category of other women's PACs that are not as adaptive, expansive, or strategic as EMILY's List. While the organization's history and internal administration keep it firmly connected to its PAC roots, the organization is clearly more than that. Rather, it is a PAC, an interest group, a party adjunct, and a campaign organization, all wrapped up into one. It is a new type of organization—a multipronged influence organization comprised of all these different types of entities working simultaneously to advance its mission.

EMILY's List: The Interest Group
In many ways, EMILY's List resembles an interest group more than a traditional PAC. PACs are considered extremely elite entities; donors may write checks, but providing money is their sole interaction with the PAC. In contrast, interest groups are membership organizations. Leaders typically serve at the pleasure of members; membership numbers rise and fall depending on the saliency of the issues and other sociopolitical factors. Most interest groups are not *primarily* political organizations— that is, they do not engage in electoral politics.[4] Instead, interest groups are organizations with a variety of resources at their disposal which use a variety of strategies to obtain their goals. Interest groups also use a variety of incentives to keep members engaged, because it is only insofar as it is representing members that an interest group has influence.

In many ways, viewing ELIST as an interest group rather than as a PAC makes more sense. As evidenced in chapter 3, EMILY's List has a variety of resources: time, money, members, patrons, a talented leader, a sophisticated support staff, patrons, and so on. It has put those varied resources to work, starting at least five new projects in the past fifteen years. Its membership has increased from 25 in 1985 to over 100,000 in 2008, in part because it offers members a variety of incentives to join. Purposive incentives come from the support the organization gives to female pro-choice Democratic candidates. Solidary incentives are obtained through the various meetings and luncheons held by the organization. Material incentives are missing, though one could argue that by giving to the organization and networking at luncheons and meetings, material benefits *could* accrue. In addition, joining the organization and supporting its endorsed candidates also provides members with an opportunity to obtain substantive, descriptive, and oftentimes geographic representation in Congress.

Over the past fifteen years, EMILY's List has even engaged in direct lobbying. In 1992 Malcolm testified in front of the Committee on House Administration regarding proposals to reform campaign finance.[5] The organization took the FEC to court regarding its enforcement of 527 regulations.[6] The organization now encourages its members to engage in grassroots lobbying, with a twist. The organization has taken an increasingly activist and partisan tone in the past few years, discussing how issues like energy, health care, employment, and gas prices, as well as stem cell research, should be issues of concern to ELIST members. When John Roberts and Samuel Alito were nominated by George W. Bush as Justices of the U.S. Supreme Court, EMILY's List came out against these nominations, posting information on its website and sending out emails to its membership. But instead of asking members to sign an online petition to forward to the appropriate member(s) of Congress (the typical example of grassroots lobbying), EMILY's List asked its members to channel their anger or excitement into writing a check in support of the organization and its candidates.

EMILY's List differs from interest groups in the strict control leaders maintain over the organization's activities. Most presidents and officers of interest groups serve at the pleasure of members or a board of directors; this is especially true of interest groups that began as part of a social movement. In these cases, the interest group represents the institutionalization of the movement, and the interest group often retains the movement's structure. For example, Barakso (2005) noted that the National Organization of Women (NOW) routinely elects a new slate of officers. The same holds true for the National Women's Political Caucus (NWPC) and many other interest groups, though the frequency of their elections and competition for the position differs, dictated in part by the organization's charter. Scholars have linked these changes in group leadership to changes in group strategy (Barakso 2005; Woods 2001). EMILY's List, however, has been able to evolve and adapt, even though one woman has led the organization for the past quarter of a century. Rather than stifle the organization, Malcolm's steady hand at the helm of EMILY's List has facilitated the organization's diversification and growth.

ELIST: The Campaign Organization
The third component of ELIST's amalgam is its function as a campaign organization. In some ways, this is what EMILY's List is best at—providing female pro-choice candidates with a full-service support network. Although EMILY's List did not start this way, by the 2000s, EMILY's List had the resources to provide its candidates with personal training, campaign staff, polling, direct mail, advertising (general issue ads and express advocacy), and phone banks, *in addition to* the contributions

it gives and bundles through its PAC activity. The quality and scope of these resources and services are unparalleled. EMILY's List now dispenses them at the federal and state/local levels, helping hundreds of female Democratic pro-choice women become members of federal and state government. The skills and resources that EMILY's List has invested in viable pro-choice Democratic female candidates has helped the Democratic Party regain or retain control of state legislatures and the U.S. Congress.

ELIST: The Party Adjunct
The final prong in the EMILY's List organization is its activity as a party adjunct. Unlike many other PACs, interest groups, and women's organizations, EMILY'S List has *always* focused its attention solely on the Democratic Party. While others hedge their bets by taking a bipartisan approach—seeking access and support from legislators on both sides of the aisle or giving money to *all* female candidates regardless of political party—EMILY's List believes that the best chance for women lies with the Democratic Party.[7] Malcolm's ties to the Democratic Party predate the creation of EMILY's List. Over the years, ties between the Party and the organization have deepened, drawing in "regular" Democratic members who sought partisan gain, bringing in top Democratic Party strategists to train candidates and campaign professionals, and hiring former Democratic Party operatives or staffers who had worked at other Democratic-leaning organizations (like the AFL-CIO).

Malcolm's desire to have EMILY's List function as a party adjunct is clear, but why would the Democratic Party find this arrangement appealing? First, by the early 1990s, EMILY's List was a premier bundler, and Malcolm became known as someone who could deliver the money that the Democratic Party desperately needed to beat the GOP. Second, the Party knew it needed women voters, and ELIST had evolved into a reference group with the ability to deliver money *and* votes. Insofar as other women's organizations were bipartisan, EMILY's List became more valuable to the Democrats. EMILY's List also began transferring money to the national and state Democratic Party organizations, spending millions on GOTV efforts that benefitted ELIST candidates, but also helped Democrats up and down the ballot by getting Democrats to the voting booth on Election Day.

The Future of EMILY's List

In classifying EMILY's List as a PAC, scholars have missed recognizing this new type of organizational form—a multipronged influence organization. While legally a PAC, ELIST is, in fact, a composite of a PAC, an interest group, a campaign organization, and a party adjunct. All of these components are critical and relevant to understanding the breadth of ELIST activity and its impact; none of them alone are determinative of that activity or impact. Hence, ELIST cannot be understood by focusing on the organization's PAC activity or its activities supporting the Democratic Party, but rather it must be understood using multiple lenses. Only then can we appreciate the story of EMILY's List as a story of strategic decision making, persistence, and power. And only then can we understand how a powerful entrepreneur and like-minded liberal feminist woman crafted a new type of political organization—a women's influence organization—with the power to change the face of politics.

If anything, the 2008 election stands as a testament to *power and the resiliency* of the organization, while also pointing to some potential limitations. The organization put its full weight and resources into Clinton's presidential campaign. As discussed in chapter 6, this brought to light the conflict between the organization and the Democratic Party. While EMILY's List is a key player in the Democratic coalition and Malcolm is viewed as a top Democratic strategist, neither the Party nor Malcolm will back down when it comes to following their beliefs (or the poll numbers). It is because of Malcolm's unwavering and unfaltering devotion to the mission of the organization that it has succeeded—she has learned from those around her and made adjustments when necessary. But when it comes to endorsing or supporting women, she does not see failure or retreat as an option.

That zeal is shared by the organization's staff and most of its membership. For those who may be attracted to the organization because of its partisan perspective and its influence, not because of its support of women or pro-choice policy, conflict between ELIST and the Party may limit their participation in the organization, as happened in 2008. Still, there is little indication that the organization suffered a permanent blow. In fact, EMILY's List was given a critical task in the post-primary season: to bring disappointed Clinton supporters back into the larger Democratic fold and help elect Senator Barack Obama as the next President of the United States. It also helped elect pro-choice Democratic women in their quest for congressional office and pro-choice Democratic women at the state and local levels.

My hope is that by explicating EMILY's List's transformation from a donor network to a multipronged influence organization, readers will understand how an organization's formal status can be helpful but also limiting to our understanding of an organization's activity and influence. It is now the task of future scholars to take our understanding of EMILY's List and its unique organizational form to the next level. That the halls of political power

Conclusion

look different because of EMILY's List cannot be disputed. Armed with the understanding of EMILY's List as an organization that evolved from a donor network into a multipronged influence organization, future scholars are now able to evaluate the policy and institutional implications of EMILY's List.

Endnotes

1. See www.senate.gov and www.house.gov. Juanita Millender-McDonald chairs the House Administration Committee, Louise Slaughter chairs the Rules Committee, and Nydia Velázquez chairs the House Small Business Committee.
2. Of the seventy-nine women currently serving in the House, only Marcy Kaptur (OH-9) and Kathy Dahlkemper (PA-3) have not received any money from EMILY's List at any point, according to data from the FEC (www.fec.gov). See also Center for American Women and Politics 2009b. As discussed in chapter 5, while all of these women may have received some level of support/endorsement from EMILY's List, that is not to say that the organization played an equally important role in all of the campaigns.
3. Although we know that EMILY's List is spending significant amounts of money at the state level, these efforts are hard to assess due to the tremendous effort needed to cull data from all the states because of differing disclosure thresholds and data-access policies.
4. The vast majority of interest groups are nonprofits 501(c)(3)s or 501(c)(4)s, whose primary mission is education, or 501(c)(5)s or 501(c)(6)s, labor unions and trade associations. If these organizations *do* engage in political activity, they do so by creating a connected PAC, known as a separate segregated fund (SSF). Connected PACs are discussed more in chapter 3.
5. U.S. Congress. House. Committee on House Administration. 1991. Hearing to review the printing chapters of Title 44 of the United States Code due to the changes in electronic information format, distribution, and technology in the past decade. 101st Cong., 1st sess., May 23.
6. *EMILY's List v. Federal Election Commission.* 569 F. Supp. 2d 18; 2008 U.S. Dist. LEXIS 58046. http://library.williams.edu/citing/styles/chicago2.php#govdoc.

7. I wonder how much of this is due to her Democratic connections with the Carter administration, how much was her observance of the position and treatment of women in the parties, and how much was position-driven, with the New Right staking claim to the GOP in the early 1980s, Reagan coming out against the ERA, and so on.

Appendix A

Coding Guide for Emily's List Mailings

1. Type of mailing
   1 = candidate recommendations; 2 = notes from EMILY/women's monitor; 3 = solicitations; 4 = majority council memos; 5 = race update; 6 = other (type in)
2. Date
3. Candidates and Races Discussed

   3a. candidate name, race (example: Louise Slaughter, NY-28)
   3b. candidate name
   3c. candidate name
   3d. candidate name
   3e. candidate name
   3f. candidate name

   If more candidates, create additional column
4. Other Races mentioned (not associated with a particular candidate)
5. Bundling Request/ ELIST programs mentioned"

   5a. Bundling Request? (asking person to send check directly to candidate?): yes = 1; no = 0
   5b. Program Name (example: Women VOTE!)
   5c. Program Name (example: POP Program)
   5d. Program Name (example: Campaign Corps)

   If more programs, create additional columns

6. If solicitation or majority council memo, who sent letter –ONLY if not Malcolm or ELIST organization, Example: Barbara Mikulski
7. Does mailing mention George Bush or Bush-Cheney (yes=1 no=0)
8. Does mailing mention Republican party (yes=1 no=0)
9. Does mailing mention John McCain (yes=1 no=0)
10. Does mailing mention other Republican or Republican group? (write name)
11. Does the mailing mention Democratic Party (yes=1 no=0)
12. Does mailing mention Nancy Pelosi (yes=1 no=0)
13. Does mailing mention other Democratic leaning organization [write name(s)], ex.: labor, Obama, Biden, etc.)
14. Does mailing mention Democratic control of Congress (yes=1 no=0)
15. If "Notes for EMILY" /"Women's Monitor" or "Race Update", title/headline on first page
16. If "Notes for EMILY" /"Women's Monitor", titles of other articles in newsletter, ex. What's Cooking? Political News from Washington and Around the Country"

   a. Titles of article(s) in newsletter
   b. Titles of article(s) in newsletter
   c. Titles of article(s) in newsletter
   d. Titles of article(s) in newsletter

   If more articles, create additional columns
17. If "Notes for EMILY" or "Women's Monitor", name of candidate spotlighted on last page
18. Are there any specific issues/policies mentioned in mailing? (yes=1, no=0)

19. If 18=yes, what issues?
- 19a. abortion
- 19b. foreign policy (Iraq, Afghanistan, etc.)
- 19c. health care
- 19d. Energy
- 19e. climate change
- 19f. Employment/jobs
- 19g. other (write in)

Appendix B

Data Collapsing and Coding

Data pertaining to the organization and its members came from records of the Federal Election Commission (FEC) and the Internal Revenue Service (IRS). As a political action committee, EMILY'S List must report financial activity to the Federal Election Commission on a monthly basis.[1] At year's end, the FEC files a yearly summary report which lists the organization's receipts, expenditures, transfers to and from the committee to and from other entities (such as candidates, the party committees, or other PACs), and the gross amount of non-federal expenditures. Data on specific types of expenditures (e.g., which candidates received what kind of support, how much the organization spent on phone banks or polling, direct mail costs, etc.) were obtained through a combination of electronic filings available as .pdf files and detail files available in database format. Data on the amount bundled to specific candidates from members came from the Federal Election Commission and Congressional Quarterly's *Political Moneyline*.

These data are critical to tracing changes in the organization and assessing how the organization used its resources to begin new projects and continue existing ones. FEC data also provided similar information on the select women's PACs as well as information on labor PAC activity and the support/recruitment the Democratic Party provided female candidates. Since 2000, when EMILY's List formed a 527, they filed yearly reports with the IRS. These 527 files are not as comprehensive because the IRS

Data Collapsing and Coding

requires a different level of disclosure; however, these files did provide information on receipts, expenditures, and transfers.

MEMBERS

The organization's monthly report to the FEC lists all contributions of $200 or more to the organization during that period including the name, city, state, zip, occupation, date, and the amount of the contribution. Also available is whether the contribution was earmarked for a specific candidate or general contribution to the organization. Those donations that were bundled were excised for separate analysis; I also created a database of individuals who only gave to the PAC.

As individuals are able to give multiple times to the organization over the course of the election cycle, and I was interested in seeing if people gave to the organization over time, I downloaded the detailed PAC file for every cycle since ELIST's formation, 1986–2008. Creating one database for each cycle, I used a series of access queries to collapse donations from the same donor. Records were only collapsed if/when there was a perfect match between the donor's last name, first three initials of his/her first name, and the zip code. This process does not account for those that moved during the cycle, not to mention those who have moved over the entire time period, however, those factors are impossible to control in a reasonable amount of time, nor is there any indication that such meticulous matching would create significantly different findings.

After checking the collapsing process, each collapsed donor in each election cycle was given a unique donor ID. These donor IDs were used to classify individuals into donor categories (described below). Before creating donor categories, I first coded the collapsed donor database for donor sex and occupation.

Sex

To code for sex, I used a series of Access queries to automatically mark donors who were identified in the FEC database as Ms., Mr., or Mrs. as female. I then ran a similar query to mark all donors identified as "Mr." as male. The remaining donors' names were then compared to a list of female first names and male first names compiled by the Census.[2] After removing names that were present in both lists, I used an Access query to compare the first name of undesignated donors to these lists. If the first name matched the name on the female list, that donor was marked as "female"; if the name matched the male list, the donor was marked "male". Those who remained were excluded from the discussion in the chapter unless mentioned specifically.

Occupation

To code for occupation, I ran a series of Access queries to code the occupation field of the FEC file for each collapsed donor. The occupation of each individual was coded into one of the following categories: Self, Home, Retired, Business, Other, Government, Legal, Education, Medical, and None.

Donor Status

To assess whether donors were Newbies or Repeaters (had given a large contribution to ELIST in a prior election cycle), each collapsed donor base was linked to the cycle before. An Access query was then run to create a table that listed the donor names and zip codes for that cycle and the donorID for that name and zip in any earlier cycle. Those coded as Newbies in that cycle did not have a donorID in any earlier cycle. Those that were Repeaters would have a DonorID for at least one earlier election cycle.

That process allowed donors in each cycle to be coded as "Newbies" or Repeaters in that cycle. Repeaters were coded into

Data Collapsing and Coding

Occasional or Loyalists. I then used an Access query to code Newbie donors in each cycle (except for 2000 and 2008) into Drop Offs (those who gave once but did not give again), Occasional, or Loyalists. The data on Drop Offs is somewhat higher than reality as the matching criteria includes zip code which means that anyone who moved to another zip code during the period would be considered a Drop Off (if the move occurred in the 2 years after their first large donation to ELIST) or an occasional donor (if they moved sometime after their second cycle of donating to the organization).

Endnotes

1. http://images.nictusa.com/cgi-bin/fecimg/?C00193433.
2. *List of Most Popular Female Names.* Accessed from http://www.census.gov/genealogy/names/dist.female.first on May 1, 2009; *List of Most Popular Male Names.* Accessed from http://www.census.gov/genealogy/names/dist.male.first on May 1, 2009.

Appendix C

Donor Breakdown According to Election Cycle and State

State	2000	2002	2004	2006	2008
CA	1381	1818	2746	2419	2329
FL	279	418	743	633	559
NY	848	1017	1525	1310	1229
OH	143	145	253	208	204
IL	272	351	564	476	454
MN	75	100	173	155	162
WI	87	99	142	131	94
PA	206	276	486	409	372
MI	129	227	347	342	255
VA	197	312	460	369	362
NJ	172	255	387	345	298
CO	115	138	269	231	280
AZ	67	114	215	193	182
MO	47	78	159	124	140
NH	29	45	82	70	73
AR	29	19	36	20	32
WA	266	246	450	415	359
CT	141	182	302	280	254
NV	21	25	42	41	41
MD	250	382	575	425	478
NC	75	91	208	153	201
OR	64	95	175	201	163
ME	22	44	77	78	64

(*continued on next page*)

State	2000	2002	2004	2006	2008
TN	26	43	75	77	60
SC	22	24	61	52	62
IA	22	26	57	51	50
WV	14	20	23	25	26
SD	3	8	11	14	7
GA	94	112	159	165	136
IN	41	45	73	71	74
KY	25	39	66	58	50
NE	11	15	24	21	23
MA	369	483	1093	701	646
TX	332	445	648	524	549
NM	59	82	108	141	112
VT	29	40	59	50	59
RI	17	22	48	47	45
HI	9	16	36	39	48
LA	24	18	34	26	31
OK	12	17	39	32	32
AL	12	17	25	20	24
MT	8	10	26	23	18
DC	297	407	506	378	403
KS	12	24	70	48	41
UT	7	35	38	39	28
DE	18	23	39	23	25
ID	5	13	24	23	20
AK	12	10	27	18	17
WY	7	12	20	16	24
MS	6	6	6	8	10
ND	2	1	1	6	4
VI	1	2	2	2	6
Blank	6	0	0	0	0
Total	6,417	8,493	13,816	11,726	11,215

REFERENCES

Abramowitz, Alan. 1995. It's abortion, stupid: Policy voting in the 1992 presidential election. *The Journal of Politics.* 57:176–186.

Aisworth, Scott. 2002. *Analyzing interests: Group influence on people and policies.* New York: W.W. Norton & Co.

Alexander, Herbert. 1984. *Financing politics: Money, elections, and political reform.* Washington, D.C.: CQ Press.

Anderson, Peggy. 1982. ERA Defeated. *Tampa Tribune.* June 24. 2.

Argyris, Chris, and David Schon. 1996. *Organizational learning II: Theory, method, and practice.* Reading, MA: Addison-Wesley.

Arnold, Laura W., and Barbara M. King. 2002. Women, committees, and institutional change. In *Women transforming Congress,* ed. Cindy Simon Rosenthal. Norman: University of Oklahoma Press.

Bai, Matt. 2005. Machine politics. *New York Times Magazine.* August 15. 11–12.

Barakso, Maryann. 2005. *Governing now.* Ithaca, NY: Cornell University Press.

Barone, Michael. 2008. *Almanac of American politics.* [S.l.]: National Journal.

———. 2009. *Almanac of American politics 2010.* [S.l.]: National Journal.

Barone, Michael, Grant Ujifusa, and Richard E. Cohen. 1997. *The almanac of American politics, 1998: The senators, the representatives, and the governors: Their records and election results, their states and districts.* Washington, D.C.: National Journal.

———. 1999. *The almanac of American politics, 2000: The senators, the representatives, and the governors: Their records and election results, their states and districts.* Washington, D.C.: National Journal.

———. 2001. *The almanac of American politics, 2002.* Washington, D.C.: National Journal.

———. 2003. *The almanac of American politics, 2004: the senators, the representatives, and the governors: Their records and election results, their states and districts.* Washington, D.C.: National Journal.

———. 2006. *The almanac of American politics, 2006: The senators, the representatives, and the governors: Their records and election results, their states and districts.* Washington, D.C.: National Journal.

Bashevkin, Sylvia. 1994. Facing a renewed right: American feminism and the Reagan/Bush challenge. *Canadian Journal of Political Science* 27: 669–698.

Benhabib, Seyla. 1995. From identity politics to social feminism: A plea for the nineties. *Philosophy of Education*, ed. Michael S. Katz, 22–36. Urbana: Philosophy Education Society.

Benson Gold, Rachel. 1980. After the Hyde Amendment: Public funding for abortion in FY 1978. *Family Planning Perspectives* 12: 131–134.

References

Bernstein, Mary. 2005. Identity politics. *Annual Review of Sociology* 31: 47–74.

Berry, Jeffrey. 1999. *The new liberalism: The rising power of citizen groups.* Washington, D.C.: Brookings.

Biersack, Robert, Paul Herrnson, and Clyde Wilcox. 1993. Seeds for success: Early money in congressional elections. *Legislative Studies Quarterly* 18: 535–551.

———. 1994. *Risky business? PAC decision making in congressional elections.* Armonk, NY: M.E. Shape.

Biersack, Robert, and Marianne H. Viray. 2005. Interest groups and federal campaign finance: The beginning of a new era. In *The interest group connection: Electioneering, lobbying, and policymaking in Washington*, 2nd ed., ed. Paul S. Herrnson, Ronald G. Shaiko, and Clyde Wilcox, 49–74. Washington, D.C.: Congressional Quarterly Press.

Boatright, Robert G. 2007. Situating the new 527 organizations in interest group theory. *The Forum* 5 (2): Article 5.

Boles, Janet. 1979. *The politics of the Equal Rights Amendment.* New York: Longman Publishers.

Brewer, Sarah. 2005. Women Campaign Consultants: A New Actor in the Campaign Process. In *Women in politics: Outsiders or insiders? : a collection of readings*, ed. Lois Duke Whitaker. 4th edition. Upper Saddle River, N.J.: Pearson Prentice Hall.

Burns, Nancy, Kay L. Schlozman, and Sidney Verba. 2001. *The private roots of public action: Gender, equality, and political participation.* Cambridge: Harvard University Press.

Burrell, Barbara. 1994. *A woman's place is in the House: Campaigning for Congress in the feminist era.* Ann Arbor: University of Michigan Press.

———. 2004. Campaign finance: Women's experience in the modern era. In *Women and elective office: Past, present, and future*, ed. Sue Thomas and Clyde Wilcox. New York: Oxford University Press. Women and political participation: a reference handbook. ABC-CLIO,

Button, James, Barbara Rienzo, and Kenneth Wald. 1997. *Private lives, public conflicts: Battles over gay rights in American communities.* Washington, D.C.: CQ Press.

Campaign Legal Center Weekly Report. 2005. Court denies EMILY's List attempt to enjoin FEC allocation rules. March 4. http://www.campaignlegalcenter.org/press-1557.html (accessed January 9, 2007).

Capek, Mary Ellen S. 1998. *Women and philanthropy: Old stereotypes, new challenges.* St. Paul: Women's Funding Network.

Carroll, Susan. 1994. *Women as candidates in American politics.* Bloomington: Indiana University Press.

Center for American Women and Politics. 2006. Women candidates for U.S. Congress. www.cawp.rutgers.edu (accessed January 3, 2007).

———. 2008a. Women presidential and vice presidential candidates: A selected list. http://www.cawp.rutgers.edu/fast_facts/levels_of_office/documents/prescand.pdf (accessed June 1, 2009).

———. 2008b. Summary of women candidates for selected offices 1970–2008: Major party nominees. http://www.cawp.rutgers.edu/fast_facts/elections/documents/can_histsum.pdf (accessed January 5, 2009).

References

———. 2009a. Women in the U.S. Congress, 1917–2009. http://www.cawp.rutgers.edu/fast_facts/levels_of_office/documents/cong.pdf (accessed June 1, 2009).

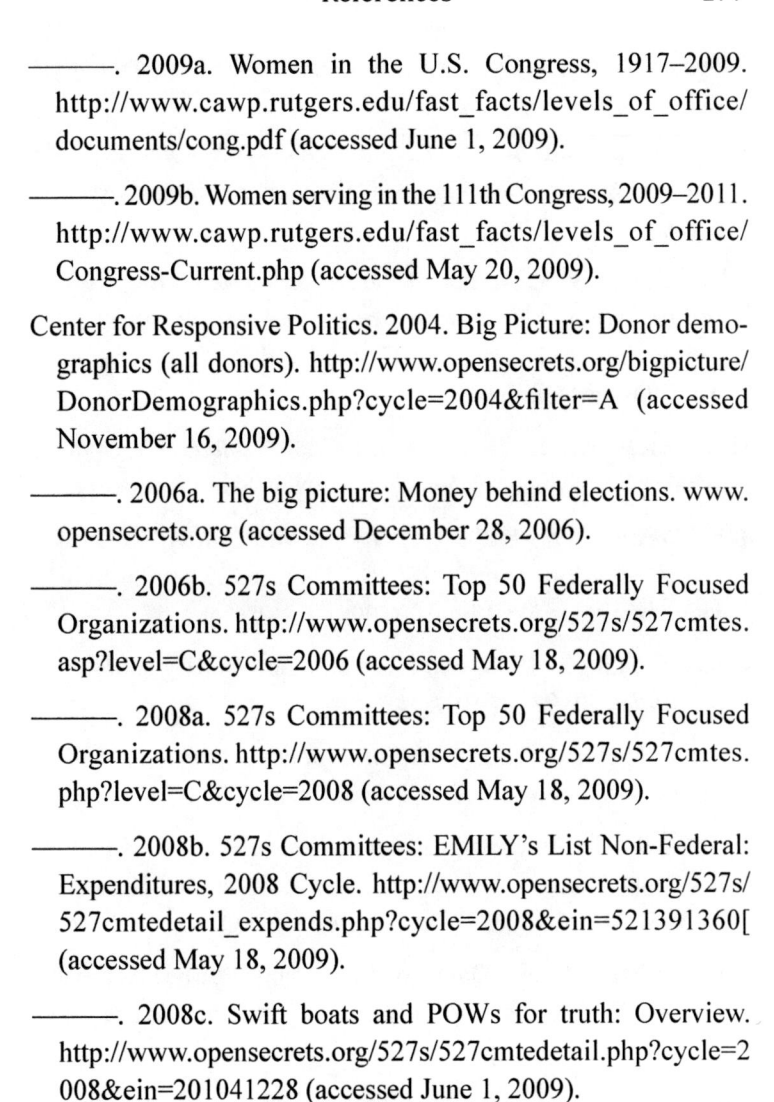

———. 2009b. Women serving in the 111th Congress, 2009–2011. http://www.cawp.rutgers.edu/fast_facts/levels_of_office/Congress-Current.php (accessed May 20, 2009).

Center for Responsive Politics. 2004. Big Picture: Donor demographics (all donors). http://www.opensecrets.org/bigpicture/DonorDemographics.php?cycle=2004&filter=A (accessed November 16, 2009).

———. 2006a. The big picture: Money behind elections. www.opensecrets.org (accessed December 28, 2006).

———. 2006b. 527s Committees: Top 50 Federally Focused Organizations. http://www.opensecrets.org/527s/527cmtes.asp?level=C&cycle=2006 (accessed May 18, 2009).

———. 2008a. 527s Committees: Top 50 Federally Focused Organizations. http://www.opensecrets.org/527s/527cmtes.php?level=C&cycle=2008 (accessed May 18, 2009).

———. 2008b. 527s Committees: EMILY's List Non-Federal: Expenditures, 2008 Cycle. http://www.opensecrets.org/527s/527cmtedetail_expends.php?cycle=2008&ein=521391360[(accessed May 18, 2009).

———. 2008c. Swift boats and POWs for truth: Overview. http://www.opensecrets.org/527s/527cmtedetail.php?cycle=2008&ein=201041228 (accessed June 1, 2009).

———. 2008d. National federation of independent business contributors. http://www.opensecrets.org/pacs/pacgave.php?cmte=C00101105&cycle=2008 (accessed January 5, 2009).

Chamblerin, Hope. 1973. *A minority of members: Women in the U.S. Congress.* New York: Praeger.

Cigler, Alan, and Burdett Loomis, eds. 2002. *Interest group politics*, 6th ed. Washington, D.C.: Congressional Quarterly Press.

Clark, Janet. 1998. Women at the national level: An update on roll call voting behavior. In *Women and elective office: Past, present, and future*, ed. Sue Thomas, and Clyde Wilcox. New York: Oxford University Press.

Clift, Eleanor, and Tom Brazaitis. 2003. *Madam president: Women blazing the leadership trail.* New York: Routledge.

CNN Special Report. 2005. Then & now: Anita Hill. June 15. http://www.cnn.com/2005/US/01/03/cnn25.tan.anita.hill/index.html (accessed June 1, 2009).

Conover, Pamela. 1988. Feminists and the gender gap. *Journal of Politics* 50: 985–1010.

Conway, M. Margaret. 1985. *Political participation in the United States.* Washington, D.C.: Congressional Quarterly Press.

———. 1991. "Interest group money in elections." In *Interest Group Politics,* 3rd ed., ed. Allan J. Cigler and Burdett A. Loomis. Washington, D.C.: Congressional Quarterly Press.

Conway, M. Margaret, David W. Ahern, and Gertrude A. Steuernagal. 2005. *Women and public policy: A revolution in progress*, 3rd ed. Washington, D.C.: CQ Press.

Cook, Elizabeth A., and Clyde Wilcox. 1991. Feminism and the gender gap: A second look. *The Journal of Politics.* 53(4): 1111–1122.

References

Cook, Elizabeth, Sue Thomas, and Clyde Wilcox. 1994. *The year of the woman: Myths & realities.* San Francisco: Westview Press.

Corrado, Anthony. 2006. Party finance in the wake of BCRA: An overview. In *Election after reform: Money, politics and the aftermath of the Bipartisan Campaign Reform Act*, ed. Michael Malbin, 19–37. New York: Rowman and Littlefield Publishers.

Costain, Anne N. 1992. *Inviting women's rebellion: A political process interpretation of the women's movement.* Baltimore: Johns Hopkins University Press.

Costantini, Edmond, and Kenneth Craik. 1977. Women as politicians: The social background, personality, and political careers of female party leaders. *Journal of Social Issues* 28(2): 217–236.

Darcy, Robert, Susan Welch, and Janet Clark. 1994. *Women, elections, and representation.* Lincoln: University of Nebraska Press.

Day, Christine, and Charles Hadley. 2001a. Who contributes? Similarities and differences between contributors to EMILY's List and WISH List. *Women & Politics* 24: 53–67.

———. 2001b. Research note: Feminist diversity: The policy preferences of women's PAC contributors. *Political Research Quarterly* 54: 673–686.

———. 2005. *Women's PACS: Abortion and elections.* Upper Saddle River, NJ: Prentice Hall.

de Figueiredo, John M., and Elizabeth Garrett. 2004. Paying for politics. *Working Paper No. 34.* Center of the Study of Law and Politics. f.n.18.

Delli Carpini, Michael X., and Ester R. Fuchs. 1993. The year of the woman? Candidates, voters, and the 1992 election. *Political Science Quarterly* 108: 29–36.

Diamond, Irene. 1977. *Sex roles in the state house*. New Haven, CT: Yale University Press.

Dodd. Lawrence. 1977. Congress and the quest for power. In *Congress reconsidered*, ed. Lawrence Dodd and Bruce Oppenheimer, 269–307. New York: Praeger.

———. 1994. Political learning and political change. In *The dynamics of American politics*, ed. Lawrence Dodd and Calvin Jillison, 311–365. Boulder, CO: Westview Press.

———. 2005. Reenvisioning Congress. In *Congress reconsidered*, 8th ed., ed. Lawrence Dodd and Bruce Oppenheimer, 411–446. Washington, D.C.: CQ Press.

Dodd, Lawrence, and Bruce Oppenheimer. 2005. A decade of Republican control: The House of Representatives, 1995–2005. In *Congress Reconsidered*, 8th ed., ed. Lawrence Dodd and Bruce Oppenheimer, 23–54. Washington, D.C.: CQ Press.

Dodson, Debra L. 1998. Representing women's interests in the U.S. House of Representatives. In *Women and elective office: Past, present, and future*, ed. Sue Thomas and Clyde Wilcox, 130–149. New York: Oxford University Press.

Dwyer, Diana, and Robin Kolodny. 2003. National political parties after BCRA. In *Life after reform: When the Bipartisan Campaign Reform Act meets politics*, ed. Michael Malbin, 83–100. New York: Rowman & Littlefield.

Echols, Alice. 1989. *Daring to be bad: Radical feminism in America, 1967–1975, American culture*. Minneapolis: University of Minnesota Press.

References

Elazar, Daniel J. 1972. *American federalism: A view from the states*. New York: Crowell.

Electronic code of federal regulations: Title 11-federal elections. http://a257.g.akamaitech.net/7/257/2422/01jan20061500/edocket.access.gpo.gov/cfr_2006/janqtr/11cfr106.6.htm (accessed March 5, 2007).

EMILY's List. n.d.[a]. WOMEN Vote! activities. http://www.emilyslist.org/programs/women_vote/activities/ (accessed on June 1, 2009).

———. n.d[b]. WOMEN VOTE! making history. http://emilyslist.org/programs/women_vote/makinghistory/index.html (accessed on July 1, 2009).

———. n.d.[c]. Women we helped elect. http://www.emilyslist.org/candidates/women-helped.html (accessed on May 30, 2009).

———. n.d.[d]. Women's monitor: Fact sheet. EMILY's List. http://www.emilyslist.org/newsroom/monitor/monitor_fact_sheet.html (accessed May 9, 2007).

———. n.d.[e]. Women's monitor. EMILY's List. http://www.emilyslist.org/newsroom/monitor/ (accessed May 9, 2007).

———. 2002. Department of the Treasury: Internal Revenue Service. http://forms.irs.gov/politicalOrgsSearch/search/generatePDF.action?formId='521391360-990POL-01'&formType=P90 (accessed May 18, 2009).

———. 2004a. About EMILY's List. November. www.emilyslist.org (accessed on December 3, 2004).

———. 2004b. Insider news. EMILY's List. http://www.emilyslist.org/happening/insider-news/20040603.html (accessed December 1, 2005).

———. 2005a. 20th Anniversary Gala Luncheon: Barbara Mikulski. EMILY's List. http://www.youtube.com/watch?v=9P5KobkPy94&feature=related (accessed May 1, 2009).

———. 2005b. 20th Anniversary Gala Luncheon: Gwen Moore. EMILY's List. http://www.youtube.com/watch?v=f40kQMo845I&feature=channel_page (accessed May 1, 2009).

———. 2005c. 20th Anniversary Gala Luncheon: Rosa DeLauro. EMILY's List. http://www.youtube.com/watch?v=aq8VheelG_0&feature=channel (accessed May 1, 2009).

———. 2007a. About Campaign Corps. EMILY's List. http://emilyslist.org/programs/campaign_corps/about/ (accessed January 5, 2009).

———. 2007b. Campaign Staff Training and Jobs. EMILY's List. http://emilyslist.org/programs/campaign_jobs/ (accessed January 5, 2009).

———. 2007c. Frequently asked questions. EMILY's List. http://www.emilyslist.org/team_emily/FAQ.html (accessed March 1, 2007).

———. 2007d. Senior leadership: Ellen R. Malcolm President and Founder. http://emilyslist.org/about/senior_leadership_malcolm/index.html (accessed January 5, 2009).

———. 2008a. Campaign Corps. EMILY's List. http://www.emilyslist.org/programs/campaign_corps/2008_campaign_corps/ (accessed January 5, 2009).

———. 2008b. EMILY's List announces new Internet director. July 14. http://emilyslist.org/news/releases/el_new_internet_director/ (accessed on June 1, 2009).

———. 2008c. EMILY's List WOMEN VOTE! begins next stage of outreach to women voters in Connecticut and New Jersey. January 25. http://emilyslist.org/news/releases/2008_connecticut_new_jersey_women_vote/ (accessed on June 1, 2009).

———. 2008d. National polling on women voters and the McCain-Palin ticket. September 3. http://emilyslist.org/news/releases/palin_poll_memo/ (accessed on June 1, 2009).

———. 2009a. EMILY's List: Latest POP victories. EMILY's List http://www.emilyslist.org/do/pop/index.html (accessed May 30, 2009).

———. 2009b. Where we come from. http://emilyslist.org/about/where_we_come_from/ (accessed October 17, 2009).

———. 2009c. Learn more about EMILY's List Majority Council. EMILY's List. http://emilyslist.org/support/majority_council/mc_learn_more/ (accessed on June 1, 2009).

Epstein, David, and Peter Zemsky. 1995. Money talks: Deterring quality challengers in congressional elections. *The American Political Science Review* 89: 295–308.

Evans, Sara. 1980. *Personal politics: The roots of women's liberation in the Civil Rights Movement and the New Left.* New York: Vintage Books.

Exemption requirements: Political organizations. 2008. Internal Revenue Service. http://www.irs.gov/charities/political/article/0,,id=96350,00.html (accessed June 1, 2009).

Faculty biography: Sean Gagen. 2009. The George Washington University: The graduate school of political management. http://www.gwu.edu/~gspm/about/bios/gagen.html (accessed January 5, 2009).

Fast facts: Gender gap in voting. 2008. Center for American Women and Politics. http://www.cawp.rutgers.edu/fast_facts/voters/gender_gap.php (accessed January 5, 2009).

Federal Election Commission. 1992. PAC financial summaries (end of cycle). http://fec.gov/finance/disclosure/ftpsum.shtml (accessed January 5, 2009).

———. 1999. Contributions received by: Participation 2000, INC. http://query.nictusa.com/cgi-bin/com_rcvd/1999_C00221887 (accessed January 5, 2009.)

———. 2000. Detailed files about candidates, parties, and other committees. October. www.fec.gov (accessed November 15, 2004).

———. 2002a. Detailed files about candidates, parties, and other committees. www.fec.gov (accessed November 15, 2004).

———. 2002b. Regulations. *Record* 28. http://www.fec.gov/pdf/record/2002/sep02.pdf (accessed October 17, 2009).

———. 2002c. Reports image index for committee ID: C00377994 (American Women Vote!). http://images.nictusa.com/cgi-bin/fecimg/?C00377994 (accessed May 1, 2009).

———. 2003. Committees and candidates supported/opposed (EMILY's List). http://query.nictusa.com/cgi-bin/com_supopp/2003_C00193433 (accessed on June 1, 2009).

———. 2004. Detailed files about candidates, parties, and other committees. October. www.fec.gov (accessed November 15, 2004).

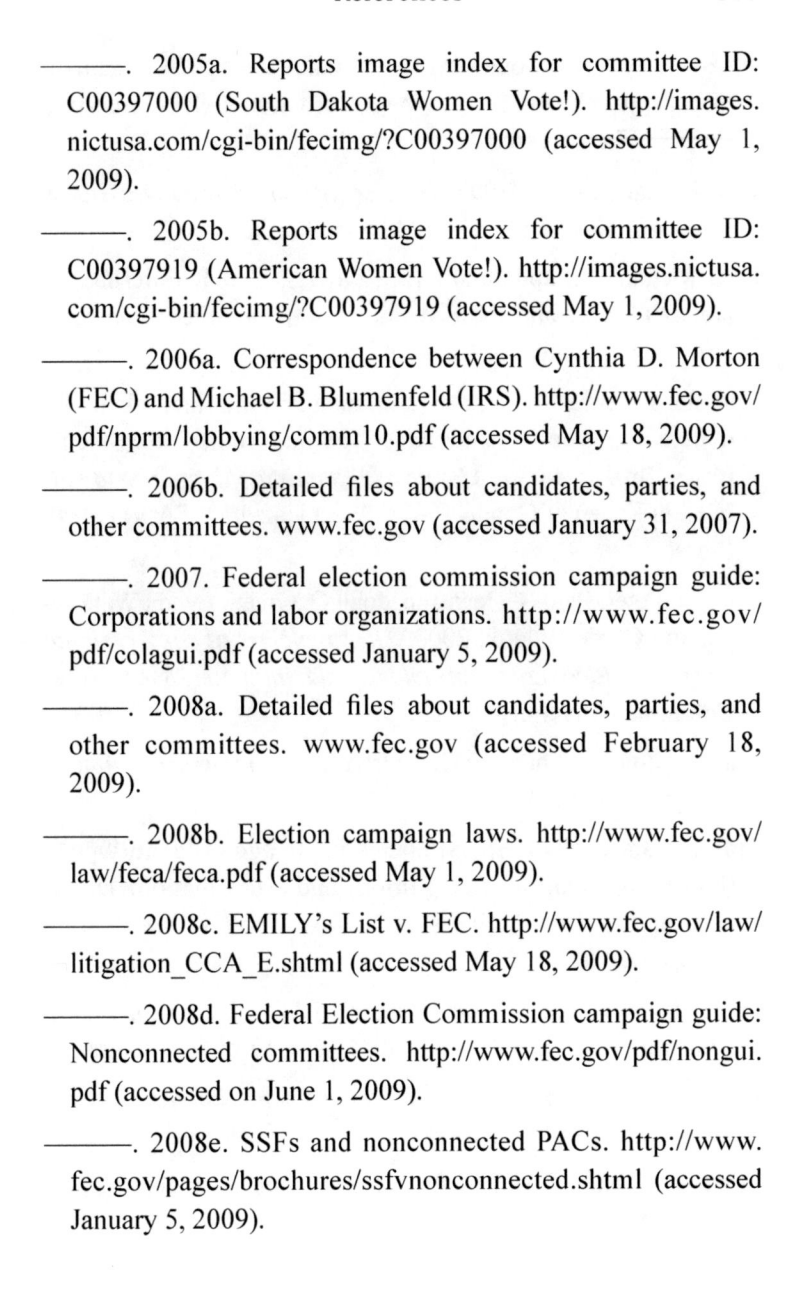

———. 2005a. Reports image index for committee ID: C00397000 (South Dakota Women Vote!). http://images.nictusa.com/cgi-bin/fecimg/?C00397000 (accessed May 1, 2009).

———. 2005b. Reports image index for committee ID: C00397919 (American Women Vote!). http://images.nictusa.com/cgi-bin/fecimg/?C00397919 (accessed May 1, 2009).

———. 2006a. Correspondence between Cynthia D. Morton (FEC) and Michael B. Blumenfeld (IRS). http://www.fec.gov/pdf/nprm/lobbying/comm10.pdf (accessed May 18, 2009).

———. 2006b. Detailed files about candidates, parties, and other committees. www.fec.gov (accessed January 31, 2007).

———. 2007. Federal election commission campaign guide: Corporations and labor organizations. http://www.fec.gov/pdf/colagui.pdf (accessed January 5, 2009).

———. 2008a. Detailed files about candidates, parties, and other committees. www.fec.gov (accessed February 18, 2009).

———. 2008b. Election campaign laws. http://www.fec.gov/law/feca/feca.pdf (accessed May 1, 2009).

———. 2008c. EMILY's List v. FEC. http://www.fec.gov/law/litigation_CCA_E.shtml (accessed May 18, 2009).

———. 2008d. Federal Election Commission campaign guide: Nonconnected committees. http://www.fec.gov/pdf/nongui.pdf (accessed on June 1, 2009).

———. 2008e. SSFs and nonconnected PACs. http://www.fec.gov/pages/brochures/ssfvnonconnected.shtml (accessed January 5, 2009).

———. 2009. Electioneering Communications: '527' organizations. http://www.fec.gov/pages/brochures/electioneering.shtml#527s (accessed June 1, 2009).

Fox, Richard Logan. 1997. *Gender dynamics in congressional elections.* Thousand Oaks, CA: Sage Publications.

Fox, Richard L., and Jennifer L. Lawless. 2004. Entering the arena? Gender and the decision to run for office. *American Journal of Political Science* 48: 264–280.

Francia, Peter. 2001. Early fundraising by nonincumbent female congressional candidates: The importance of women's PACs. In *Women and Congress: Running, winning, and ruling,* ed. Karen O'Connor, 7–20. West Hazelton, PA: Haworth Press.

Francia, Peter, Paul S. Herrnson, John C. Green, Lynda W. Powell, and Clyde Wilcox. 2003. *The financiers of congressional elections: Ideologues, investors, and intimates.* New York: Columbia University Press.

Franke-Guta, Garance. 2003. EMILY'S List hissed. *The American Prospect* 13: 12–3.

Fraser, Nancy. 1996. Social justice in the age of identity politics: Redistribution, recognition, and participation. Delivered at Stanford University: *Tanner Lectures on Human Values*.

Fredrickson, Heather. 2004. Women's PACs: Their motivation, strategies, and impacts. Ph.D. diss. West Virginia University.

Freeman, Jo. 1975. *The politics of women's liberation.* New York: Longman Publishers.

Friedman, Jon. 1993. The founding mother. *New York Times.* May 2: 50

Gais, Thomas. 1996. *Improper influence: Campaign finance law, political interest groups, and the problem of equality.* Ann Arbor: The University of Michigan Press.

Gertzog, Irwin. 1995. *Congressional women: Their recruitment, integration, and behavior.* 2nd ed. New York: Praeger.

Giddings, Paula. 1984. *When and where I enter: The impact of black women on race and sex in America.* New York: William Morrow and Company, Inc.

Githens, Marianne, and Jewel Prestage. 1977. *Portrait of marginality.* New York: D. McKay Co.

Glaze, Mark. 2005. Court denies EMILY's List attempt to enjoin FEC allocation rules. February 25. http://www.campaignlegalcenter.org/press-1551.html (accessed November 25, 2006).

Goldstein, David. 2008. What's the future for McCaskill, Obama's friend, advocate? *McClatchy.* November 17. http://www.mcclatchydc.com/homepage/story/55916.html (accessed on June 1, 2009).

Green, John C., and Nathan S. Bigelow. 2005. The Christian right goes to Washington: Social movement resources and the legislative process. In *The interest group connection: Electioneering, lobbying, and policymaking in Washington.* 2nd ed., ed. Paul S. Herrnson, Ronald G. Shaiko, and Clyde Wilcox, 189–211. Washington, D.C.: CQ Press.

Green, John C., and James L. Guth. 1991. Religion, representatives and roll calls. *Legislative Studies Quarterly* 15: 571–581.

Green, John, Paul Herrnson, Lynda Powell, and Clyde Wilcox. 1999. *Report: Women big donors mobilized in congressional elections.* June 8. http://www.bsos.umd.edu/gvpt/herrnson/women.html (accessed August 1, 2006).

Grenzke, Janet. 1989. PACs and the congressional supermarket: The currency is complex." *American Journal of Political Science* 33: 1–24.

———. 2004. *Women and power on Capitol Hill: Reconstructing the congressional women's caucus.* Boulder, CO: Lynne Rienner Publishers.

Grogan, David. 1992. For whom the bell tolls. *People* 37:19.

Guth, James, and John Green. 1991. An ideology of rights: Support for civil liberties among political activists. *Political Behavior* 13: 321–344.

Hanisch, Carol. 1969. The personal is political. In *Feminist Revolution.* New York: Penguin.

Hays, Constance. 1992. Trends collide in 3rd district rematch. *The New York Times.* October 31. 23.

Herrnson, Paul S. 2005. Interest groups and campaigns: The electoral connection. In *The interest group connection: Electioneering, lobbying, and policymaking in Washington*, 2nd ed., ed. Paul S. Herrnson, Ronald G. Shaiko, and Clyde Wilcox, 25–48. Washington, D.C.: Congressional Quarterly Press.

Hill, David. 1981. Political culture and female political representation. *The Journal of Politics* 43: 159–168.

Hogan, Robert. 2001. The influence of state and district conditions on the representation of women in U.S. state legislatures. *American Politics Research* 29: 4–24.

References

Hoover Institution. n.d. Public policy inquiry: Campaign finance: Supreme Court cases. http://www.campaignfinancesite.org/court/buckley1.html (accessed October 17, 2009).

The Houston Chronicle. 1992. PAC for women expects no monetary payback. December 20. A4.

Huddy, Leonie, and Nayda Terkildsen. 1993. Gender stereotypes and the perception of male and female candidates. *American Journal of Political Science* 37: 119–147.

Internal Revenue Service. n.d. Form 8771. Department of the Treasury: Internal Revenue Service. http://forms.irs.gov/politicalOrgsSearch/search/Print.action?formId=4771&formType=6E71 (accessed May 18, 2009).

Institute for Politics, Democracy & the Internet, and the Campaign Finance Institute. 2006. Small donors and online giving: A study of donors to the 2004 presidential campaigns. March. http://www.ipdi.org/UploadedFiles/Small%20Donors%20Report.pdf.

Jacobson, Gary. 1980. *Money in congressional elections.* New Haven, CT: Yale University Press.

———. 2003. Terror, terrain, and turnout: Explaining the 2002 midterm elections. *Political Science Quarterly* 118: 1–22.

Jaquette, Jane S. 1997. Women in power: From tokenism to critical mass. *Foreign Policy* 108: 23–37.

Jewell, Sandra. 2003. EMILY's List: Is it over between us? May 23. http://www.commondreams.org/views03/0515-01.htm (accessed April 5, 2006).

Kahn, Kim Fridkin. 1996. *The political consequences of being a woman.* New York: Columbia University Press.

Kathlene, Lyn. 2001. Words that matter. In *The impact of women in public office*, ed. Susan B. Carroll, 22–48. Bloomington: Indiana University Press.

Kaufmann, Karen, and John Petrocik. 1999. The changing politics of American men: Understanding the sources of the gender gap. *American Journal of Political Science* 43: 864–887.

Koenenn, Connie. 1992. Taking a step off the platform politics: Disgruntled with their party's anti-abortion stance, Republican women launch a grass-roots fund-raising network to elect likeminded female candidates. *Los Angeles Times*. April 2. 14.

Kornacki, Steve. 2006. Men are from Mars, women are from .... Mars?: Gender roles in 21st century campaigns. *Campaigns and Elections* 28: 40–42.

Kim, Thomas P. 1998. Clarence Thomas and the politicization of candidate gender in the 1992 Senate elections. *Legislative Studies Quarterly* 23: 399–418.

Kincaid, Diana. 1978. Over his dead body: A positive perspective on widows in the U.S. Congress. *Western Political Quarterly* 31: 96–104.

Kirkpatrick, Jeane. 1974. *Political women*. New York: Basic Books.

Klein, Ethel. 1984. *Gender politics: From consciousness to mass politics*. Cambridge, MA: Harvard University Press.

Krasno, Jonathan, and Donald Green. 1988. Preempting quality challengers in House elections. *Journal of Politics* 50: 920–936.

Lee, Marcia Manning. 1977. Toward understanding why few women hold public office: Factors affecting the participation of

References

women in local politics. In *A portrait of marginality: The political behavior of the American woman*, ed. Marianne Githens and Jewel L. Prestage, 118–178. New York: David McKay.

Lorber, Judith. 2005. *Gender inequality: Feminist theories and politics*. 3rd ed. Los Angeles: Roxbury.

Magee, Christopher. 2002. Do political action committees give money to candidates for electoral or influence motives? *Public Choice* 112: 373–399.

Mahood, H. R. 2000. *Interest groups in American politics*. Upper Saddle River, NJ: Prentice Hall.

Malbin, Michael J. 1980. *Parties, interest groups, and campaign finance laws*. Washington, D.C.: American Enterprise Institute for Public Policy Research.

———. 2003. Thinking about reform. In *Life after reform: When the Bipartisan Campaign Reform Act meets politics*, ed. Michael Malbin, 3–20. New York: Rowman & Littlefield.

———. 2004. Political parties under the post-McConnell Bipartisan Campaign Reform Act. *Election Law Journal* 3: 177–191.

———. 2006. Assessing the Bipartisan Campaign Reform Act. In *Election after reform: Money, politics, and the Bipartisan Campaign Reform Act*, ed. Michael Malbin, 1–18.

Malbin, Michael J., and Thomas Gais. 1998. *A day after reform: Sobering campaign finance lessons from the American states*. Washington, D.C.: Brookings.

Malcolm, Ellen R. 2007. Endorsing Sen. Hillary Clinton for president. January 20. http://emilyslist.org/news/releases/2008_clinton_endorsement/ (accessed May 1, 2009).

———. 2008a. Statement from Ellen R. Malcolm on NARAL endorsement in the Democratic presidential primary. May 14. http://emilyslist.org/news/releases/2008_naral_endorsement_malcolm_statement/ (accessed on June 1, 2009).

———. 2008b. Statement from Ellen R. Malcolm on Ellen Moran as President-elect Obama's White House communications director. November 22. http://emilyslist.org/news/releases/20081122_moran_comm_dir/ (accessed on June 1, 2009).

———. 2009. Statement on the ruling in EMILY's List v. FEC. September 18. http://emilyslist.org/news/releases/2009_EL_FEC_ruling/ (accessed September 28, 2009).

Mansbridge, Jane. 1985. Myth and reality: The ERA and the gender gap in the 1980 election. *Public Opinion Quarterly* 49: 164–78.

———. 1986. *Why we lost the ERA*. Chicago: University of Chicago Press.

Massachusetts congressional delegation: U.S. Senators. AllLaw.Com. http://www.alllaw.com/state_resources/Massachusetts/congress/default.asp (accessed on June 1, 2009).

McClusky, Tim. 2009. Change watch backgrounder: Ellen Moran. February 18. http://www.frcblog.com/2009/02/change-watch-backgrounder-ellen-moran/ (accessed on June 1, 2009).

McCormick, Jon. 2008. McCaskill backs Obama. *The Swamp*. January 11. http://www.swamppolitics.com/news/politics/blog/2008/01/mccaskill_endorses_obama.html (accessed on June 1, 2009).

McGlen, Nancy E., and Karen O'Connor. 1983. *Women's rights: The struggle for equality in the nineteenth and twentieth centuries*. New York: Praeger.

Moe, Terry A. 1980. Calculus of group membership. *American Journal of Political Science* 24: 593–632.

Mueller, Carol McClurg. 1988. *The Politics of the gender gap: The social construction of political influence.* Newbury Park, CA: SAGE Publications.

Murray, Shailagh. 2008. At daughter's urging, McCaskill backs Obama. *The Washington Post.* January 13. http://blog.washingtonpost.com/44/2008/01/13/at_daughters_urging_mccaskill.html (accessed March 3, 2008).

NARAL Pro-Choice America. 2006. Results for endorsed candidates. November. www.prochoiceamerica.org (accessed January 3, 2007).

National Organization for Women. 2009. About NOW. http://www.now.org/about.html (accessed January 5, 2009).

National Institute on Money in State Politics. 2009. http://www.followthemoney.org/index.phtml (accessed November 16, 2009).

National Public Radio interview with Former Sen. Carol Moseley Braun. 2003. National Public Radio. http://www.npr.org/programs/specials/democrats2004/braun.html (accessed on June 1, 2009).

National Public Radio. 2004. Braun ends candidacy, supports Dean. January 15. http://www.npr.org/templates/story/story.php?storyId=1600149 (accessed on June 1, 2009).

National Public Radio: Morning Edition. 2007. McAuliffe: Shorter 2008 race speeds fundraising. http://www.npr.org/templates/story/story.php?storyId=7292720&sc=emaf (accessed January 5, 2009).

National Right to Life News. 2001. If EMILY's List supports a candidate, what does that tell you? June.

Nechemias, Carol. 1987. Changes in the election of women to U.S. state legislative seats. *Legislative Studies Quarterly* 12: 125–142.

Office of Federal Relations: California congressional delegation roster, 111th Congress. 2009. The California State University. http://www.calstate.edu/FederalRelations/roster.shtml (accessed on May 1, 2009).

Olson, Mancur. 1965. *The logic of collective action.* Princeton: Yale University Press.

Ornstein, Norman, and Shirley Elder. 1978. *Interest groups, lobbying, and policy-making.* Washington, D.C.: Congressional Quarterly.

Ornstein, Norman, Thomas Mann, and Michael Malbin. 2002. *Vital statistics on Congress 2000–2001.* Washington, D.C.: The AEI Press.

———. 2008. *Vital statistics on Congress.* Washington, D.C.: Brookings Institution Press.

Overby, Peter. 2007. Independent groups target Iowa, New Hampshire. National Public Radio. December 7. http://www.npr.org/templates/story/story.php?storyId=16996409 (accessed on July 1, 2009).

Patterson, Kelly D., and Matthew M. Singer. 2002. The National Rifle Association in the face of the Clinton challenge. In *Interest group politics*, ed. Allan J. Cigler and Burdett A. Loomis, 55–77. Washington, D.C.: CQ Press.

Paley, Marian L. 1993. Elections 1992 and the Thomas appointment. *Political Science and Politics* 26: 28–31.

References

Pappu, Sridhar. 2008. EMILY's List in the aftermath. *The Washington Independent*. http://washingtonindependent.com/1059 (accessed May 25, 2009).

Pimlott, Jamie. 2006. Pulling in the dough: Contribution patterns of EMILY's List donors. Presented at the *American Political Science Association Conference*, Philadelphia.

Political Moneyline. 1986. PAC/party profile search. www.fecinfo.com (accessed January 5, 2007).

———. 1988. PAC/party profile search. www.fecinfo.com (accessed January 5, 2007).

———. 1990. PAC/party profile search. www.fecinfo.com (accessed January 5, 2007).

———. 1992. PAC/party profile search. www.fecinfo.com (accessed January 5, 2007).

———. 1994. PAC/party profile search. www.fecinfo.com (accessed January 5, 2007).

———. 1996. PAC/party profile search. www.fecinfo.com (accessed January 5, 2007).

———. 1998. PAC/party profile search. www.fecinfo.com (accessed January 5, 2007).

———. 2000. PAC/party profile search. www.fecinfo.com (accessed January 5, 2007).

———. 2002a. PAC/party profile search. www.fecinfo.com (accessed January 5, 2007).

———. 2002b. Report for EMILY's List Non-Federal. www.fecinfo.com (accessed August 2006).

———. 2004a. PAC/party profile search. www.fecinfo.com (accessed January 5, 2007).

———. 2004b. Report for EMILY's List Non-Federal. www.fecinfo.com (accessed August 2006).

———. 2006a. PAC/party profile search. www.fecinfo.com (accessed June 7, 2007).

———. 2006b. Report for EMILY's List Non-Federal. www.fecinfo.com (accessed June 1, 2007).

———. 2008. PAC/party profile search. www.fecinfo.com (accessed April 1, 2009).

Poole, Keith, and Howard Rosenthal. 1997. *Congress: A political-economic history of roll call voting.* London: Oxford Press.

Reingold, Beth. 1992. Concepts of representation among female and male state legislators. *Legislative Studies Quarterly* 17: 509–537.

Reynolds, Catherine. 2004. SC voters may have gotten incorrect information. *Associated Press Wire.* http://www.wistv.com/global/story.asp?s=2509824&ClientType=Printable (accessed March 1, 2009).

Roberston, John A. 1992. Casey and the resuscitation of *Roe v. Wade. The Hastings Center Report* 22: 24–28.

Rosenthal, Cindy. 1998. *When women lead: Integrative leadership in state legislature.* New York: Oxford University Press.

Rozell, Mark J., and Clyde Wilcox. 1999. *Interest groups in American campaigns: The new face of electioneering.* Washington, D.C.: CQ Press.

Russakoff, Dale. 2004. Democracy-to-go: Contested states are magnets to droves of mobile activists. *The Washington Post.* October 24.

Ryan, Barbara. 2001. *Identity politics in the women's movement.* New York: New York University Press.

Sabato, Larry. 1981. *The rise of political consultants: New ways of winning elections.* New York: Basic Books.

———. 1984. *PAC power: Inside the world of political action committees.* New York: W.W. Norton & Company.

Salisbury, Robert. 1992. *Interests and institutions: Substance and structure in American politics.* Pittsburgh: University of Pittsburgh Press.

Slavin, Sarah. 1995. *US women's interest groups: Institutional profiles.* Westport, CT: Greenwood Press.

Sanbonmatsu, Kira. 2002. Political parties and the recruitment of women to state legislatures. *The Journal of Politics* 64: 791–809.

———. 2004. *Democrats, Republicans, and the politics of women's place.* Ann Arbor: University of Michigan Press.

Sanchez, Julian. 2004. Politicizing the Web. *Reason* 36: 13.

Sapiro, Virginia. 1983. *The political integration of women: Roles, socialization, and politics.* Urbana: University of Illinois Press.

Schattschneider, E. E. 1975. *Semisovereign people: A realist's view of democracy in America.* Hinsdale, IL: Dryden Press.

Schlozman, Kay, and Carol Uhlaner. 1986. Candidate gender and congressional campaign receipts. *Journal of Politics* 48: 30–50.

Schlozman, Kay Lehman, Nancy Burns, and Sidney Verba. 1999. 'What happened at work today?': A multistage model of gender, employment, and political participation. *The Journal of Politics* 61(1): 29.

Schwawrtz, Maralee, and Kenneth Cooper. 1992. Female candidates got major boost from contributors. *The Washington Post.* November 8.

Semiatin, Richard J., and Mark J. Rozell. 2005. Interest groups in congressional elections. In *Interest group connection*, 2nd ed., ed. Paul Hernnson, Ronald Shaiko, and Clyde Wilcox, 75–88. Washington, D.C.: Congressional Quarterly Press.

Smith, Richard A. 1995. Interest group influence in the U.S. Congress. *Legislative Studies Quarterly* 20: 89–139.

Snow, David E., Bourke Rochford, Jr., Stephen K. Worden, and Robert D. Benford. 1986. Frame alignment processes, micromobilization, and movement participation. *American Sociological Review* 51: 464–481.

Sorauf, Frank. 1984. *What price PACs?* New York: The Fund.

———. 1992. *Inside campaign finance: Myths and realities.* New Haven, CT: Yale University Press.

Spake, Amanda. 1988. Women can be power brokers, too: How Ellen Malcolm learned to influence elections and love it. *The Washington Post.* June 5. 22.

Swers, Michelle. 2001a. *The difference women make: The policy impact of women in Congress.* London: University of Chicago Press.

———. 2001b. Research on women in legislatures: What have we learned, where are we going? *Women & Politics* 23: 167–185.

Taylor, Catharine P. 2004. Campaign aides. *MediaWeek* 14: 18–20.

Taylor, Verta. 1989. Social movement continuity: Women's movement in abeyance. *American Sociological Review* 54: 761–775.

References

Tauscher, Ellen O. 1997. Bipartisan freshmen task force on campaign finance reform to convene first hearing. April 24. http://www.house.gov/tauscher/press/4-24-97.htm (accessed April 2006).

Thomas, Ken. 2004. EMILY's List program trains women to run for office. *Associated Press State & Local Wire*. May 25.

Thomas, Stephen W. 1978. Commentaries. In *Parties, interest groups and campaign finance laws*, ed. Michael J. Malbin, 82–85. AEI symposia, 79I. Washington: American Enterprise Institute for Public Policy Research.

Thomas, Sue. 1994. *How women legislate*. New York: Oxford University Press.

Tolchin, Susan, and Martin Tolchin. 1974. *Clout: Womanpower and politics*. New York: Coward, McCann & Geoghegan.

United States: State population estimates. 2008. U.S. Census Bureau. http://factfinder.census.gov/servlet/GCTTable?_bm=y&-geo_id=01000US&-_box_head_nbr=GCT-T1-R&-ds_name=PEP_2008_EST&-_lang=en&-format=US-40S&-_sse=on (accessed on June 1, 2009).

Vaida, Bara, and Jennifer Skalka. 2008. Can EMILY's List get its mojo back? *National Journal Magazine*. June 28. http://www.nationaljournal.com/njmagazine/cs_20080628_6871.php (accessed May 15, 2009).

Verba, Sidney, Kay Schlozman, and Henry E. Brady. 1995. *Voice and equality: Civic voluntarism in American politics*. Cambridge: Harvard University Press.

Walker, Jack. 1991. *Mobilizing interest groups in America: Patrons, professions, and social movements*. Ann Arbor: University of Michigan Press.

Walsh, Katherine Cramer. 2002. Enlarging representation: Women bringing marginalized perspectives to floor debate. In *Women transforming Congress*, ed. Cindy Simon Rosenthal. Norman: University of Oklahoma Press.

Walsh, Mark. 2004. Using the Web the way Dean did. *Business Week*. http://www.businessweek.com/magazine/content/04_35/c3897005_mz003.htm#ZZZJTBQESXD (accessed December 1, 2005).

Women's Campaign Fund. 2009. WCF overview. http://www.wcfonline.org/sn/overview (accessed January 5, 2009).

Weisberg, Jacob. 1992. Ellen Malcolm: The woman behind those women candidates. *The Sunday Oregonian*. November 2. L07.

Weissman, Steven, and Kara Ryan. 2006. *Nonprofit interest groups' election activities and federal campaign finance policy: A working paper.* July. http://www.cfinst.org/books_reports/pdf/NonprofitsWorkingPaper.pdf (accessed July 25, 2006).

Weissman, Steve, and Ruth Hassan. 2006. BCRA and the 527 groups. In *The election after reform: Money, politics and the Bipartisan Campaign Reform Act*, ed. Michael Malbin, 79–111. Lanham, MD: Rowman and Littlefield.

Welch, Susan, Margery M. Ambrosius, Janet Clark, and Robert Darcy. 1985. The effect of candidate gender on electoral outcomes in state legislative races. *The Western Political Quarterly* 38: 464–475.

Wilson, James Q. 1973. *Political organizations*. New York: Basic Books.

Wilson, Marie C. 2004. *Closing the leadership gap: Why women can and must help run the world*. New York: Penguin.

Witt, Linda, Glenna Matthews, and Karen Paget. 1994. *Running as a woman: Gender and power in American politics*. New York: Free Press.

Women are gaining and exercising power in all facets of their lives. 1997. *About Women & Marketing* 10 (Sept. 30): 9.

Women's Monitor. 2008. From 18 to 80: Women on politics and society. http://emilyslist.org/multimedia/18_to_80/ (accessed on June 1, 2009).

Woods, Harriet. 2001. *Stepping up to power: The political journey of American women*. Boulder, CO: Westview Press.

Zeleny, J. 2003. Braun faces cash-strapped reality. *Chicago Tribune.* May 21. 8.

Index

527s, 5, 69–72, 82n55, 83n60, 141, 154

Abramowitz, Alan, 46
Abzug, Bella, 19
Alito, Samuel, 154
America Coming Together (ACT), 75, 106

Barakso, Maryann, 7, 19, 24, 32, 81n46, 112n8, 155
Bashevkin, Sylvia, 24
Benson Gold, Rachel, 42
Biersack, Robert, 35, 40n23, 57
Bigelow, Nathan S., 61
BIPAC, 35, 39n14
Bipartisan Campaign Reform Act (BCRA), 105, 114n18
Boatright, Robert G., 70
Boxer, Barbara, 147
Braun, Carol Mosley, 136–137, 146n1
Brazaitas, Tom, 26, 60, 146n3
Brewer, Sarah, xiii, 46
bundling, 11n2, 28–29, 14n18. *See also* EMILY's List, bundling
Burns, Nancy, 63, 88, 95
Burrell, Barbara, 11n1, 22, 32, 35, 43–44, 47, 57
Bush, George H. W., 24
Bush, George W. 62, 137, 154

Cahill, Mary Beth, 49, 138
campaign finance
  brokers, 28–29
  direct contributions, 5, 16, 29, 54–56, 143, 151–152
  early money, 47, 57, 79n25
  in-kind contributions, 5, 16, 29, 54–56, 137, 151–152
  independent expenditures, 5, 16–17, 54, 115n27, 137, 151
  issue advocacy, 33, 72
  soft money, 2, 33, 65–66, 70, 105
Campaign Finance Institute, xiv, 112n6
candidates
  challenger, 22, 36, 47, 59, 117–131
  credibility, 48–51
  incumbents, 22, 36, 44, 47, 62, 118–133, 136, 149
  open seat candidates, 44, 47, 59, 117–120, 123, 125, 131
  patrons, 61, 121, 132, 154
Capek, Mary Ellen, 115n28
Carroll, Susan, 44
Carter, Jimmy, 26, 161n7
Center for American Women and Politics, 11n6, 25, 39n13, 39n16, 40nn17–18, 42, 58, 77n2, 77n4, 78n13, 79n28, 102, 118, 136, 160n2

Center for Responsive Politics,
    11n2, 39n10, 70, 82n54,
    83n59, 83n62, 88, 111n6, 120
Cheney, Richard, 62
Chisholm, Shirley, 19–20
Clift, Eleanor 26, 60, 146n3
Clinton, Hillary Rodham, 1–2,
    9, 62, 73, 108, 132, 135,
    138–145, 146n6, 147–148,
    158
Common Cause, 26
competitive elections, 22,
    101–103, 121–122, 125
Conway, M. Margaret, xiii,
    39n15, 57, 77n5, 80n38
congressional donors, 80n36,
    88–89
Congressional Quarterly, 56,
    102–103, 111n1, 112n12,
    122–123, 128
Conover, Pamela, 106
Cook, Elizabeth, 106
Cooper, Kenneth, 77n1
COPE, 35, 39n14, 40n23. *See
    also* lead PACs
Corrado, Anthony, 105
cost of campaigning, 20–21
Costain, Anne, 7, 15, 24, 32

Day, Christine, 28, 35, 87, 93,
    111n2, 113n14, 140
de Figueiredo, John M., 111n5
DeLauro, Rosa, 53, 78n18,
    79n23, 147
Democratic Party, 4–5, 32–37,
    42, 44, 47, 49, 51–52, 64–65,
    69, 74–76, 86, 95, 104,

Democratic Party (*continued*)
    116n30, 123–125, 129,
    136–140, 143–144, 148,
    156–158
descriptive representation, 26,
    36, 47
Dodd, Lawrence C., xiii–xiv, 72

Elder, Shirley, 15
elections
    of 1986, 30–31, 42, 50–51,
        53, 55–56, 66, 150
    of 1988, 4, 30–31, 33, 40–50,
        56, 66, 132
    of 1990, 30–31, 33, 42, 44,
        50, 56, 66–67
    of 1992, 7, 30–31, 38n7,
        42–48, 50, 56, 60, 66,
        77n1, 77n3, 136
    of 1994, 30–31, 34, 50,
        55–56, 64–66
    of 1996, 4, 30–31, 34, 40n23,
        50–51, 56, 64–67, 78, 87,
        89, 111n2
    of 1998, 30–31, 34, 56,
        65–67, 136
    of 2000, 29–31, 34, 40n23,
        49, 56–58, 65–67, 72,
        92–94, 96–102, 104, 108,
        118–120, 124, 126–132
    of 2002, 29–31, 34, 47, 56,
        58, 61, 65–68, 70–72,
        81n43, 83n58, 94, 99–100,
        104–105, 107–109,
        113n13, 118–119,
        124–126, 129–130

elections (*continued*)
  of 2004, 21, 29–35, 56–58, 65–74, 94, 99–100, 104–109, 111n1, 111n6, 113n13, 118–119, 124–126, 128–130, 137–138
  of 2006, 2, 29–31, 34, 56–58, 65–68, 70–72, 94, 99–100, 104–109, 113n13, 118–119, 124–126, 128–130, 139, 142–144
  of 2008, 1–3, 9, 18, 30–31, 34, 38, 50–51, 56–58, 61–62, 65–68, 70–73, 87–88, 92–94, 96–100, 102, 104–105, 107–108, 112n12, 113n13, 115n29, 116n29, 118–120, 124–130, 134–145, 146n6, 157–158
EMILY's List
  bundling, 2–3, 5, 28–29, 31, 60, 152–153
  Campaign Corps, 48–49, 77nn8–10, 151
  candidate viability, 8, 25, 52–53, 59–60, 78n15, 120–121, 126, 137–138, 150
  descriptive representation or goals, 26, 36–37, 42, 47, 64, 70, 103, 110, 154
  donor network, 1, 5, 18, 27–28, 37, 42, 52, 70–71, 86, 95, 144, 158–159
  early money, 1, 4–5, 9, 26, 47, 52, 56–59, 79n25

EMILY's List (*continued*)
  endorsement, 1–2, 9, 20, 35–37, 44, 51–62, 72, 78n1, 91, 101, 103, 106, 108, 116n30, 117–133, 135, 138–139, 142–143, 150–152, 160n2
  Facebook, 73, 84n65
  Founding Mothers, xiii, 4, 13, 26, 32, 36, 42, 45, 52, 54, 75, 79n24, 86, 95, 137, 150
  GOTV activity, 62. *See also* WOMEN VOTE!
  helping candidates be competitive, 26, 44–52, 56–57, 73
  lobbying, 5, 15, 19, 154
  mailings, 54–55, 61–63, 91–92, 150
  Majority Council, 91, 112n7
  membership
    demographics, 85–104
    Loyalists, 93, 104, 108–109
    material benefits, 38n6, 89–90, 154
    Newbies, 105–110
    occasional donors, 89–93, 108–110
    purposive benefits, 90–91, 103, 154
    solidary benefits, 90–91, 103, 154
  multipronged women's influence organization, 3, 5, 9, 18, 37, 48, 85–86, 95,

EMILY's List (*continued*)
104, 132, 142, 144, 148,
151–153, 157–159
non-federal activity, 5, 35,
66–72, 81n45, 82n53,
83n62
phone banks, 141, 155
Political Opportunity
Program, 5, 62–68, 82n48,
82n51
polling, 56, 143, 155
presidential elections, 1–2,
9–10, 62, 69–72, 108, 132,
135–145, 148, 158
primary activities, 2, 9, 27,
47, 57–60, 75, 79n28, 103,
108, 134n2, 139, 142–144,
158
role of competition in
endorsement, 53, 79n28,
101–103, 121–122,
125–126, 128–133,
151–152
strategic decision making, 3,
27, 51, 60–61, 64, 69, 86,
118, 128, 138, 150–153,
157
TEAM EMILY, 40n22,
72–73, 84n64
WOMEN VOTE!, 1, 4,
34, 62–68, 75, 80n42,
81nn43–44, 82n53, 138,
141, 143
women-versus-women races,
59–61
Women's Monitor, 4, 64,
80nn39–40, 143, 151

Epstein, David, 47
Equal Rights Amendment
(ERA), 4, 23–26, 36–37,
41–43, 127, 131, 161n7
Federal Election Campaign
Act (FECA), 14–16, 20, 33,
38n3, 41, 114n18
Federal Election Commission
(FEC), 11n6, 17, 33, 38n4,
38n7, 39n8, 39n9, 39n14, 66,
70–73, 77n3, 78n12, 78n14,
80n41, 82n55, 83n57, 83n60,
85, 92, 97, 111n1, 112nn10–11,
113n14, 113nn16–17,
114n22, 115n27, 121, 134n3,
142–143, 146n5, 149, 151,
154, 160n2
Feinstein, Dianne, 147
Ferraro, Geraldine, 60, 137
Fox, Richard Logan, 46
Francia, Peter, 8, 47, 57, 63,
80n36, 87–89, 95, 104,
113n16, 114n18, 134n2
Freeman, Jo, 13, 19, 39n15
Friedman, Jon, 98

Gais, Thomas, 101
gender gap, 20–23, 39n16, 63,
85, 88, 149
gender stereotypes, 46
geographic representation, 103,
110, 154
Gertzog, Irwin, 22
get-out-the-vote (GOTV), 2, 4,
17, 33, 35, 40n23, 44, 62,
65, 67, 71, 101, 106, 115n25,

Index

get-out-the-vote (GOTV) (*continued*) 116n30, 151, 157. *See also* EMILY's List, WOMEN VOTE!
Giddings, Paula, 20
Goldstein, David, , 140
Green, John C., , 61, 63, 87–89
Grogan, David, 43

Hadley, Charles, 28, 35, 87, 93, 111n2, 113n14, 140
Hassan, Ruth, 72
Herrnson, Paul, 36, 165
Hill, Anita, 42–43
Howes, Joanne, 32, 40n20, 78n19, 79n24, 95, 113n15, 146n3
Huddy, Leonie, 47

identity politics, 6, 37, 76, 87, 149
Internal Revenue Service, 71, 83n56, 83n58, 83nn60–61

Kahn, Kim Fridkin, 45
Kaufmann, Karen, 106
Kerry, John, 49, 137–138
King, Barbara M., 163
Kolodny, Robin, 33
Kornacki, Steve, 46, 48

Labor organizations, 14, 17, 33, 35, 39n9, 45, 82n55, 90, 123, 148, 160n4
Landrieu, Mary Beth, 139
lead PACs, 35–36. *See also* COPE and BIPAC

liberal feminist women's movement, 6–7, 13, 24–26, 94, 142, 144, 149, 157
Lichtman, Judith, 78n19, 79n24, 146n3, 146n6
Limbaugh, Rush, 62
Lincoln, Blanche, 139
Lorber, Judith, 87, 111n3
Lowey, Nita, 61, 77n1

Magee, Christopher, 22
Malbin, Michael J., xiv, 22, 26–27, 55, 85, 101, 104, 108, 125
Malcolm, Ellen, 1–6, 11n3, 13–14, 26–29, 31–37, 40n19, 42–44, 47–48, 52–54, 61–64, 67, 70–75, 85, 97, 103, 111n4, 130–132, 139–142, 144–145, 146n6, 149–150, 154–158
Mann, Thomas, 22, 26, 55, 125
Mansbridge, Jane, 25
Matthews, Glenna, 44–46
McCaskill, Claire, 139–142
McClusky, Tim, 139
McCormick, Jon, 140
McGlen, Nancy E., xiii, 39n15, 94
Mikulski, Barbara, 51, 61, 79n23, 86, 150
Miss America Pageant of 1968, 13
Moe, Terry, 90
Mondale, Walter, 137
Moore, Gwen, 61, 79n23
Moran, Ellen, 145

Mueller, Carol McClurg, 39n15
Murray, Shailagh, 144

National Abortion Rights Action League (NARAL), 141–142
National Institute on Money in State Politics, 112n6
National Organization of Women (NOW), 18, 34, 39n11, 81n46, 94, 112n8, 155
National Public Radio (NPR), 78n15, 136–137, 146n1
National Right to Life News, 139
National Women's Political Caucus (NWPC), 7, 14, 19–21, 30–32, 39n14, 41–43, 81n46, 155
NFIB PAC, 18
Nixon, Richard, 15

O'Connor, Karen, xiii, 39n15, 94
Obama, Barack, 139–141, 144, 148, 158
Oliver, Ramona, 52, 60, 74, 78n16, 78n19, 80n29, 84nn66–68, 146n4
Olson, Mancur, 90, 149
Ornstein, Norman, 22, 26, 55, 125
Overby, Peter, 140

Paget, Karen, 44–46
Pappu, Sridhar, 108
Partial Birth Abortion Ban, 139
Participation 2000, 49, 77n10
Patterson, Kelly D., 61
Pelosi, Nancy, 62, 132, 147
Petrocik, John, 106

political action committees (PACs)
 access strategy, 22
 connected, 17–20, 29, 38, 71, 160n4
 non-connected, 3, 17–18, 29, 71, 81, 91, 152
political equality, 88
Political Moneyline, 31, 56, 78n14, 111n1, 112n12
political participation, 23, 88
pro-choice, 2, 4–5, 8, 31, 36–37, 42–43, 49, 51–54, 57, 59–60, 62, 68, 123, 127, 130–133, 135, 138–139, 148, 151–152, 154–158

Reagan, Ronald, 24, 41, 161
Richards, Ann, 67
Roberts, John, 154
Robertson, John A., 42
Roe v. Wade (1973), 53–54, 135, 141–142
Russakoff, Dale, 35
Ryan, Kara, xiv

Sabato, Larry, 14–16, 27–28, 38n6, 80n37
Sanbonmatsu, Kira, 35
Sanchez, Julian, 73
Sapiro, Virginia, 39
Schattschneider, E. E., 14
Schlozman, Kay L., 88, 165
Schroeder, Patricia, 136–137
Schwawrtz, Maralee, 77n1
Semiatin, Richard J., 40n23
Singer, Matthew M., 61

Index

Skalka, Jennifer, 2, 140, 144
Slavin, Sarah, 19
Snow, David E., 64
Sorauf, Frank, 14–18, 28–29, 33, 38n2, 149
Spake, Amanda, 5, 32, 38n1
stealth PACs, 69. *See also* 527s
Stegall, Lael, 27
substantive representation, 36–37, 42, 64, 70, 103, 110, 154
Sununu, John, 62
Swift Boat Veterans for Truth, 69–70, 82n54

Taylor, Catharine P., 73
Taylor, Verta, 24
Terkildsen, Nayda, 47
Thomas, Clarence, 42–43
Thomas, Ken, 69
Thomas, Stephen W., 17, 29, 36
Tolchin, Martin, 23
Tolchin, Susan, 23
Tupperware Party, 3–4, 11n1, 14, 42, 76

U.S. Congress, 3, 6, 8–9, 15, 23, 25, 28–29, 40n17, 42–43, 51–52, 55, 61, 79n27, 80n30, 101–102, 111n4, 114n24, 120–122, 127, 131–133, 147–148, 154–156, 160n5
    House of Representatives, 11n6, 25–26, 49, 55,

U.S. Congress (*continued*)
    57–59, 63, 65, 78n15, 118–119, 122–123, 128–129, 132, 147, 154, 160nn1–2, 160n5
    Senate, 25–26, 55, 57–59, 118–119, 125, 128–129, 147, 160n1
U.S. Supreme Court, 38n3, 42, 141–142, 154

Vaida, Bara, 2, 140, 144
Verba, Sidney, 88
Viray, Marianne, 35–36, 40n23

Walker, Jack, 61, 90
Walsh, Mark, 73
Weissman, Steven, 72
White House, 2–3, 6, 24, 62, 136, 145
Wilcox, Clyde, 106
Wilson, James Q., 90
Windom Fund, 26–27
Witt, Linda, 44–46
Women's Campaign Fund (WCF), 7, 14, 19–21, 31–34, 39n12, 39n14, 41–43, 190
women's PAC, 7, 14, 18–37, 41–43, 66–67, 71, 87, 111n2, 123, 138, 148, 153, 169, 176
Woods, Harriet, 26, 32, 37, 43, 81, 155

Year of the Woman, 44

Zeleny, J., 137
Zemsky, Peter, 47

LaVergne, TN USA
07 October 2010
199880LV00003B/4/P